D30:
EXERCISES FOR DESIGNERS

D30:
EXERCISES FOR DESIGNERS

Jim Krause

HOW
BOOKS

Cincinnati, Ohio
www.howdesign.com

For more excellent books and resources for designers, visit www.howdesign.com.

17 16 15 14 13   5 4 3 2 1

ISBN-13: 978-1-4403-2395-9

Distributed in Canada by Fraser Direct
100 Armstrong Avenue
Georgetown, Ontario, Canada L7G 5S4
Tel: (905) 877-4411

Distributed in the U.K. and Europe by F&W Media International, LTD
Brunel House, Forde Close, Newton Abbot, TQ12 4PU, UK
Tel: (+44) 1626 323200, Fax: (+44) 1626 323319
Email: enquiries@fwmedia.com

Distributed in Australia by Capricorn Link
P.O. Box 704, Windsor, NSW 2756 Australia
Tel: (02) 4560-1600

Editor: Scott Francis
Art director: Claudean Wheeler
Production coordinator: Greg Nock

About the author:

Jim Krause has worked as a designer/illustrator/photographer
in the Pacific Northwest since the 1980s. He has produced award-
winning work for clients large and small and is the author and creator
of over a dozen books for creative professionals, including *Idea Index*,
Layout Index, *Color Index*, *Color Index 2*, *Typography Index*, *Design Basics Index*,
Photo Idea Index, *Photo Idea Index: People*, *Photo Idea Index: Places*,
Photo Idea Index: Things and *The Logo Brainstorm Book*.

WWW.JIMKRAUSEDESIGN.COM

TABLE OF CONTENTS

INTRODUCTION

Creative exercises for designers and other art-minded people.

Thank you for picking up a copy of my latest book, *D30*. It's a book that I've wanted to do for a long time and it's one that I'm particularly happy with now that it's finished.

The book's title, by the way, is shorthand for thirty days' worth of creative exercises for designers. Do you have to be a designer to use this book? Not at all. Anyone interested in art and creativity could get plenty from this book's art, design, drawing, painting, photography and writing exercises. Do you have to complete the book's exercises in thirty days? Ha. Are you kidding—who has that kind of control over their schedule? This book, in spite of the fairly specific nature of its title, makes no demands about who uses it, how it is used, or how quickly it is finished (or even if it's finished at all).

The purpose of each project in *D30* is the same: to awaken, energize and exercise creative parts of our beings in ways that can be directly applied to both personal and professional creative projects. Another thing that each of the book's projects has in common is that they are fun. Take my word for this—I spent the last eighteen months developing and trying out the book's exercises myself and I can honestly say that I can't remember a time when I've had this much fun working for a living. Go ahead: Take a quick look through the book's images, and ask yourself, *Does this look like fun, or what?*

Most of the activities in *D30* involve hands-on media like pens, pencils, paints and paper. Be assured that the book's emphasis on hands-on tools and materials is not meant to downplay the relevance and the value of digital media. Not by a long shot. In fact, every exercise in the book is designed to boost the reader's art sense in ways that can be applied to media of any sort: digital or non. So, why is this book's emphasis on non-digital media? It's simply because we spend more than enough time on both the creating and the receiving end of cyber media in our daily lives, and this book will give you what may well be a much-needed chance to unplug and to re-experience what happens when your brain, eyes, arms, hands, fingers and senses are given the chance to roll up their sleeves (both figuratively and otherwise) and dive into real-world art projects without any sort of digital aids or restrictions. You may be surprised how good this feels, how well it works in teaching and emphasizing art concepts and techniques and—very importantly—how enjoyable it is.

The look of the book.
D30 is printed in black and white. This is no accident—and it has nothing to do with pinching pennies (though truth be told, it probably did save you more than a few pennies on the book's asking price). The reason the book is printed in black and white—and not in full color— is simple: Colors can be highly influential, and because *D30* is designed to inspire far more than it is to influence, its images are presented in monochrome so that you will be all the more inclined to use colors of your choosing when working on the book's projects.

Tips and some words of advice.

- Before beginning any of *D30*'s activities, read the project's instructions from start to finish. This should only take a few minutes and it will inform you about what you'll be doing (and when) and will help you avoid running into delays and dead ends as you work.

- There is an advantage to doing the book's exercises in order, since some of the earlier exercises contain elements that relate to later ones. If you'd rather skip around and do things non-numerically, that would be okay, too, but still make a point of beginning with Activity #1 (page 10) since this project is specifically designed to precede all the others.

- Think of the outcome of each of the book's activities as a beginning rather than an end. Look at everything you create and think, *What could I do with what I've learned here? How could this be applied to my own projects? Where could I take this and how far could I go?*

- Feel free to depart from the book's instructions and samples whenever the mood strikes: No bonus points are being awarded for following this book's instructions to the letter.

- *D30* has a web resource: WWW.JIMKRAUSEDESIGN.COM/**D30**. A few digital samples are posted there, as is late-breaking news regarding the book's content.

Thanks again for choosing *D30*. I would love to hear from you and see samples of what you create through the book's exercises—there's a "contact" link at the above web address.

Jim Krause

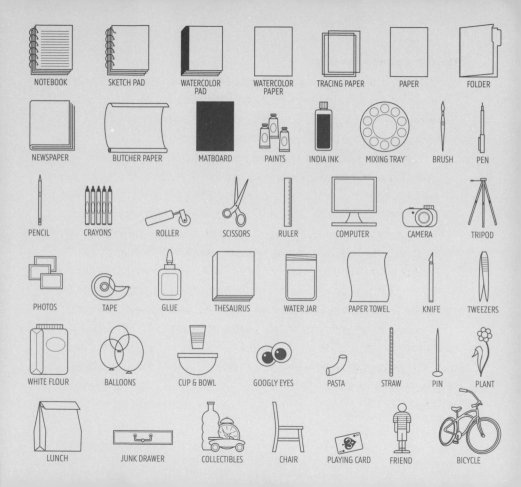

NOTEBOOK

SKETCH PAD

WATERCOLOR PAD

WATERCOLOR PAPER

TRACING PAPER

PAPER

FOLDER

NEWSPAPER

BUTCHER PAPER

MATBOARD

PAINTS

INDIA INK

MIXING TRAY

BRUSH

PEN

PENCIL

CRAYONS

ROLLER

SCISSORS

RULER

COMPUTER

CAMERA

TRIPOD

PHOTOS

TAPE

GLUE

THESAURUS

WATER JAR

PAPER TOWEL

KNIFE

TWEEZERS

WHITE FLOUR

BALLOONS

CUP & BOWL

GOOGLY EYES

PASTA

STRAW

PIN

PLANT

LUNCH

JUNK DRAWER

COLLECTIBLES

CHAIR

PLAYING CARD

FRIEND

BICYCLE

SUPPLIES

Not all of the supplies shown at left will be needed for this book's projects, and many of the must-have supplies will be easily found around your home or office. Other essentials (mentioned ahead) can be purchased at an art store, an office supply store or an online outlet. To help avoid delays when you turn to new projects, consider collecting most or all of the following supplies before you begin the book's activities.

NOTEBOOK   SKETCH PAD   WATERCOLOR PAD   WATERCOLOR PAPER   BUTCHER PAPER   TRACING PAPER (OPTIONAL)

PAPERS

In addition to ordinary letter-size pieces of paper, there are six other kinds of paper that will be used for the book's projects. A **notebook** with ruled pages will be used for pen-and-paper brainstorming activities. A **sketch pad** will be ideal for drawing projects and for developing thumbnail sketches. Pick up a 5"×8" or a 7"×10" **watercolor pad** for the book's ink and paint exercises (if you already have larger sheets of watercolor paper, then you could cut pieces from those). **Butcher paper** will be used for both art projects and to protect work surfaces. Consider also purchasing a letter-size pad of **tracing paper** for projects that involve developing visuals with pencil.

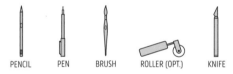

PENCIL PEN BRUSH ROLLER (OPT.) KNIFE

WRITING, PAINTING, PRINTMAKING AND CUTTING TOOLS

A wooden or mechanical **pencil** will be used throughout the book, as will an ordinary **pen**. Several activities call for **paint brushes** (inexpensive #2 and #5 watercolor brushes would work fine). An optional tool is a small **ink roller** that could be used for the printmaking exercise on page 50. If you don't already have an **X-Acto** knife, be sure to buy one since it will used for many of the projects.

PAINTS INDIA INK PAINT MIXING TRAY

PAINTS AND INK

Each of the paints used for this book's activities are water soluble. A set of **watercolors** should be purchased, and the paints could be in "cake" form (usually sold in plastic trays or metal tins) or they could be in tubes. **Gouache** is a type of opaque watercolor sold in tubes, and a set of these will be handy for some of the exercises (upper-quality gouache can be expensive, so consider buying a student grade set). A starter set of **acrylics** might also come in handy, but the watercolors and gouaches already mentioned should cover all the book's painting needs. **India ink** will be used for two or three projects (eight-ounce squeeze-top bottles of India ink are usually priced much more economically than smaller containers). A plastic or metal **paint mixing tray** will be used in several projects. *A reminder: Protect your clothing and work surfaces when working with paints and inks.*

CAMERA   COMPUTER

CAMERAS AND COMPUTERS

Digital cameras are used for several of the book's projects. Anything from a smartphone camera to a pocket-sized shooter to a DSLR will work nicely. Computers will be used on occasion as well—laptop or desktop. Also called for will be software such as Adobe's Illustrator and Photoshop (or Photoshop's junior relative, Elements), along with basic video editing software. (If you're lucky, a video editing program came packaged with your recently bought computer or camera. Free and cheap video software is also available online. If you don't have a computer or access to programs like these, consider borrowing equipment from a friend or a coworker.)

Activities

CONVERSATION WITH SELF, PART I. Welcome to the first project in *D30*. This exercise will not only help clarify artistic goals that have been floating around in your head for months or years, it will also bring new creative intentions and ideals to mind. Another great thing about this pen-and-paper brainstorming activity is that it will send all this information to the fore of your brain where it will be ready to connect with the ideas and discoveries that come up as you work on this book's activities. Got a pen? Paper? A timer of some kind? Excellent. You are ready to begin.

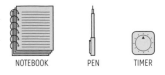

NOTEBOOK   PEN   TIMER

Activity 1: Conversation with self, part 1. Leave your laptop alone for this exercise: Writing with pen and paper will help lend this brainstorming session the thoughtful and deliberate pace it deserves. What about doing this activity in a cozy living room chair, on the front porch, on a park bench or at a coffee shop? Bring a timer (smartphone app or otherwise) with you.

First of all, congratulations on not skipping this exercise just because it doesn't involve using colorful craft supplies or your digital camera. Just know that there will be plenty of that sort of thing ahead, and by doing this exercise, you will be doubly prepared to make the most of the upcoming art-producing projects.

The goal of this activity is twofold. For starters, you'll be asked to come up with an assessment of your skills—both in terms of what you are good at and what you want to be good at. After that, you'll be building a written compilation of creativity-based goals and ideals you'd enjoy seeing in the future. And, as mentioned in this activity's intro, giving thought to these things before you begin this book's exercises will do you a real favor: It will pre-program your brain to look for ways of using what you learn and experience through the exercises to help you reach—and expand—your creative objectives.

Begin this project by deciding, firmly, that the next hour is reserved for this brainstorming project. No phone calls, no Internet, no texting, no nothing. Just you, a pen, a notebook, a timer and a brain that's ready to storm.

Next, make yourself comfortable and do whatever you need to do to set aside the day's distractions, obligations, excitements, disappointments and worries. How about taking a few deep breaths and a well deserved pause before starting?

Set your timer for fifteen minutes. This is how long you'll be writing for the first part of the exercise. Using an audible timer—instead of a visual clock—will help you avoid the temptation of constantly looking at the clock as you work.

13

Put pen to paper and write about what you are good at. Write down anything and everything that comes to mind. Don't just write about things related to art and creativity: If you are good at fixing cars, write about it; and if you are also good with mathematics and can bake an incredible pecan pie, write down a thing or two about those talents as well. The main point here is to keep

your pen moving as steadily as possible and to keep your train of thought flowing for the entire fifteen minutes. Add details to things you've already written if new ideas begin to run thin.

When you hear the timer sound, finish whatever thoughts (if any) you still need to put down, take a short pause and get ready for the next part of the project.

Set your timer for twenty minutes and begin part two by writing about improvements you'd like to see in the talents you possess. Write about talents you would like to develop from scratch as well. Jot down thoughts related to—

and apart from—artistic interests. Work diligently at this until you hear the timer go off (and, by all means, continue beyond this time if ideas are flowing).

The final segment of this activity is relatively wide open, and the instructions are simple: Set your timer for twenty-five minutes and start writing about specific visions—both small and large—of what you would love to see happening in your creatively-oriented future. For example, you could write about a collection of your photographs or paintings you would like to see in a downtown gallery; you could pen some thoughts about a website or a book you would like to see posted or published; or you could record some specific ideas about what you would especially like to see yourself doing for a living.

The first few things you write about may have been swimming around in your head for years. That's great. Write a few sentences about these subjects. After that, reach hard for new material and keep in mind as you write that there are no bad ideas when brainstorming: Just keep your thoughts flowing and the pen moving.

One powerful tactic to employ at this point is to look for opportunities for creative cross-pollination between things you wrote about in this exercise's earlier segments. For example, what if you were to blend your natural pie-making prowess with your photographic savvy to create a gorgeous blog filled with mouth-watering images and articles on the art of baking? Or what if you combined your ability to handle a welding torch with your eye for composition and created a series of stainless steel abstract sculptures? Brainstorm the possibilities deeply and thoughtfully: The most compelling art projects are often those that blend seemingly unrelated ideas and media.

Keep at this until your timer tells you that time is up, and even then, don't stop unless you feel fully ready to wrap things up.

Finish this exercise by sealing your handwritten pages in an envelope. Put the envelope in a place where it will be out of sight but not lost: You'll be asked to open this envelope after you've made your way through all (or most) of the book's projects and have reached the final exercise on page 238.

What we learn
to do, we learn
by doing. ARISTOTLE

Activity
2

SWIRLING SWIRLS. Consider this project an introduction to a doodling habit you can undertake whenever you find yourself with pen, paper and a few minutes to spare. Not only will this habit develop hand skills, it will also improve your eyes' ability to evaluate curves and compositions as you create decorative panels of swirls (filigree that could be enjoyed for what it is and/or saved for future professional projects). Unsure about your ability to gracefully render this activity's designs? Don't worry about it: Simply aim for a consistent look for each curve, line and dot you create—the beauty of your creations may surprise you.

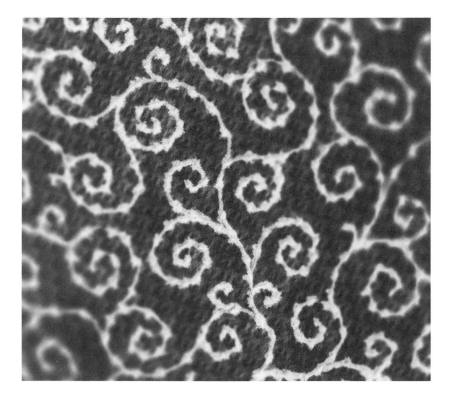

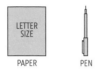

LETTER SIZE PAPER

PEN

Activity 2: Swirling swirls. A letter-size sheet of ordinary paper will work for this exercise, but feel free to use better quality paper if you like. A fine or an extra-fine tipped rollerball pen would be ideal, but other kinds of pens will suffice as well—including whatever pen happens to be floating around in a nearby drawer, purse or shoulder bag.

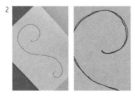

① Fold your letter-size sheet of paper into quarters. ② Next, visualize how a double-ended swirl will look within one of the quarter-sheet panels. Rehearse your stroke a few times without touching pen to paper. Then, when you're ready, draw the swirl with confidence and grace. After you've drawn the swirl, follow it backwards with the pen to double its line (this will give your swirl a more casual appearance while allowing you to make subtle corrections to its form).

③ Add a couple more swirls to your first. Rehearse each line before rendering it; draw all new swirls as if they were growing from previous lines; vary the sizes of your swirls; retrace all lines from end to beginning (just as you did in step 2); keep the swirls relatively large for now—smaller curls will be added as the work progresses.

④ Continue adding a variety of large and medium swirls until the panel is filled. ⑤ Add smaller and smaller swirls to the panel while maintaining a consistent and balanced coverage of decor.

Move to another of your paper's panels and give yourself a fresh start if you start feeling frustrated with the design you're creating.

How about finishing things off by inserting clusters of berries or flowers within your design's open spaces? What about adding tiny leaves or thorns to the design's swirling vines? Can you think of anything else that could be added to your creation to enhance its look?

Feeling inspired? Fill another of your paper's panels with a design that has a radically different visual personality. How about a design based on squares or triangles? Or a mix of shapes?

Try drawing swirls with a rollerball pen or a felt-tipped pen on absorbent paper. Allow the pen to pause frequently as you work so that its ink spreads into small splotches. This design was drawn with a fine-tipped rollerball pen on a paper napkin.

Consider using software to finalize the look of your hand-drawn designs. Here, Photoshop has been employed to convert the previous image into a panel of high-contrast filigree.

What can you do with your new-found talent once you get the hang of creating swirling swirls and other kinds of ornate decorations? You could: decorate a paper cafe napkin to impress a date; spiff up a sheet of cheap butcher paper for use as decorative gift wrap; scribe filigree in the sand during low tide; add eye-catching flourishes to a note addressed to a friend or a coworker; spontaneously craft the perfect backdrop for a last-minute design project; apply show-stopping pastry decorations to party cupcakes; add gorgeous designs to curtains or cushions using fabric paint; apply decorative colored chalk to the walkway in front of your home or apartment; squirt ketchup onto a plate of fries in an unusually ornate manner; artistically render a set of temporary tattoos for a special event.

Activity
3

CATEGORY:
DIMENSIONAL

GOING FOR THE GOLDSWORTHY.

Ever hear of Andy Goldsworthy? Have you seen the *Rivers and Tides?* It is a documentary made in 2001 that features Mr. Goldsworthy's outdoor sculptures and on-site visual arrangements made from things like twigs, branches, leaves, rocks and icicles. If you haven't seen it, consider watching—or at least looking online for photos of this artist's meticulously crafted works— in preparation for this activity's projects. Hopefully, this investigation will ignite a strong impulse to grab a coat, a lunch (and possibly a friend) for a spontaneous and creatively themed outdoor excursion.

LUNCH   CAMERA   FRIEND (OPT.)

Activity 3: Going for the Goldsworthy. A lunch, appropriate clothing and a camera are all you'll need for this activity. For your work area, choose an interesting urban or natural environment where you'll be able to gather things like rocks, sticks or leaves. And consider bringing a friend with you— someone with a kindred yearning to create a spontaneous work of art.

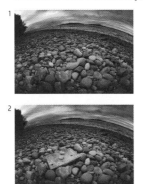

What follows is a play-by-play of a Goldsorthy-like outdoor endeavor. Use this narrative to give you ideas for a similar project of your own.
① A beach, empty of everything except for rocks and refuse: the perfect canvas for an on-site art project. ② A small steel plate is carried from the water's edge for use as the creation's centerpiece. Two white-and-black speckled rocks sit on top of the plate: A decision has been made to collect and use this kind of rock for the creative work that will follow.

TIME NEEDED:
AT LEAST A COUPLE OF HOURS

③+④ The collecting continues until a significant pile of speckled stones has been found and transported to the work area. ⑤ After spending a few minutes pondering the possibilities, it is decided to arrange the stones in a linear path that will contrast with the naturally random arrangement of rocks on which it will sit. The assemblage begins to take shape.

No matter what objects you use for your on-site creation, and no matter how you choose to arrange this material, put everything you know about design, composition, art and conveyances into play as you incorporate each item into your improvisational work of art.

29

6

⑥ The final result is just one of an infinite number of on-site dimensional creations that could have been built in this place on this day. What to do next? Snap some pictures, of course. The photos taken of artful assemblages like this will remain long after the tide, wind and rain gradually return the building blocks of your creation to their natural state of beautiful disorder.

The beach is a great place to go for this kind of creative work/play. So is a forest, a desert, a field, a vacant parking lot, an empty playground or your backyard. Not only is this a great "planned" creative exercise, it's also something you can do on a whim when you find yourself in a right place at a right time.

Goldsworthy-like creations need not be created
on a large scale. Here, a tidy collection of small
banded rocks (rocks that were stumbled upon
while searching for the main project's black-and-
white specimens) have been arranged into a
nest-like ensemble atop a bed of seaweed.

Environmental sculptures don't have to be created outdoors. What about spending a rainy afternoon inside creating dimensional compositions from household items?

An enjoyable afternoon was spent combining espresso cups and coffee beans (both whole and ground, and both brewed and unbrewed) for these visual assemblages. The arrangements seen here were created on a kitchen countertop and photographed using natural light.

WRONGS MAKING RIGHT. What's wrong with this portrait? Let's count the ways: It's overexposed, it's blurry, and compositionally, there's an awful lot of empty space in the middle of the shot. And wait, aren't the subject's eyes closed, too? They say that two wrongs don't make a right, but what about three, four or five wrongs? Could this many wrongs ever be right? When it comes to communicative and contemporary photos, the answer is an emphatic *yes*. (For proof, just take a look at the expressive photos commonly used for forward-thinking book covers, trendy magazine articles and mood-inspiring ads.) Enough said: Fetch a camera and start turning wrongs into rights.

CAMERA

COMPUTER
& PHOTOSHOP

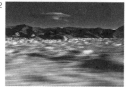
HELPER/MODEL
(OPT.)

Activity 4: Wrongs making right. A camera that offers control over focus, exposure, shutter speed and aperture size would be perfect for this activity—after all, the more control a camera offers, the more its controls can be "mishandled" in order to invite so-called imperfections. Use Photoshop or other image-editing software to finalize the look of your images.

① How about taking a camera with you on a photographic field trip for this activity? Head out to a photo-rich environment such as a downtown area or a place of natural wonders and start taking pictures. Here's the one rule: Make a point of doing something "wrong" with each and every photo you snap. ② How about selecting a slow shutter speed and taking a photo from the passenger seat of fast-moving car?

TIME NEEDED:
AN HOUR OR TWO

③ What about composing a shot with an over-abundance of empty space? A photo like this can be especially useful to designers since it offers all kinds of open space for things like text or other visuals. ④ If you snap a photo that's technically wrong, consider bringing it into Photoshop and—if anything—boosting its flaws. Photoshop's **CURVES** controls were used to brighten the already too-light areas of this image while bringing depth and darkness into its shaded areas.

Think twice about deleting photos simply because they are too dark, too light, or poorly focused. Who knows, these shots may be the real winners from a day of picture-taking.

3

4

Above: The overexposed areas of this shot don't seem to be problem. Further "flaws" were introduced by blurring the scene's perimeter. ⑤ Too dark for detail? How about capturing a dramatic silhouette? ⑥ And then there's the trick of waving the camera around while photographing city lights at night.

Push the limits with this project: See how many wrongs you can put into photos while still coming up with compelling and communicative images.

Ever heard of a Lensbaby? Lensbabies are funny little lenses that attach to digital SLRs and allow users to capture beautifully flawed photos—images that look as though they might have been shot with an old-time plastic-lens camera.

Activity
5

THE VALUE OF VALUES. Fine artists have a saying: *If the value is wrong, the color can't be right.* What does this mean? It's simple: No matter how beautiful a color is, or how carefully it has been muted and blended, it's not going to look right if it is too dark or too light. Period. Being able to see and evaluate values is an extremely important skill to possess whether you are an artist, a designer, a decorator or a photographer. Not only will this exercise strengthen your ability to discern a color's value while ignoring potentially distracting factors such as its hue and saturation, it will also give you the chance to spend some quality time with paper and paints.

COLOR TERMINOLOGY

HUE
means color. Red, green, yellow and blue are hues. So are orange, violet, brown, teal, chartreuse and any other color you can imagine.

SATURATION
Is the intensity of a hue. A saturated hue is a color in its purest form. A desaturated hue is a muted or grayed-out version of a color.

VALUE
refers to how light or how dark a hue is in comparison to a scale that goes from white to black. The importance of values is demonstrated by the role they play in painted portraits: Artists can freely shuffle a portrait's hues and levels of saturation while maintaining recognizable and attractive renderings of their subjects, but things will become a mess in a real hurry if an artist's subject is rendered with values that are even slightly off target.

WATERCOLOR PAD PENCIL BRUSH GOUACHE OR ACRYLICS PAINT MIXING TRAY WATER JAR RAG OR PAPER TOWEL

Activity 5: The value of values. For this project you'll need a pad or a sheet of watercolor paper, a pencil, a fine-tipped brush, tubes of gouache (a type of opaque watercolor or acrylic paint) or regular acrylics, a tray for mixing colors, a jar of water and a rag. Access to a computer and a printer would also be helpful but is not mandatory.

① Gather your supplies and find a well-lit place to work. Gouache would be ideal for this exercise since the colors mixed for this project should be opaque. Regular acrylics would also work as long as you keep them as opaque as possible by limiting the amount of water or medium you add to the paint (a touch of titanium white in a color's mix also helps with the opacity of acrylics).

TIME NEEDED:
AN HOUR OR TWO

② Got access to a computer and a printer? If so, copy this grayscale strip and print it down the middle of a white sheet of paper. You'll be testing swatches of color beginning in step five by painting them onto different segments of the strip and then matching the colors' values with the printed grays.*

Don't have access to a computer and printer? Use the printed grayscale shown here, and instead of painting on top of the strip, apply your paint swatches to the edge of a piece of paper and hold them next to this grayscale for evaluation.

③ Next, create this pencilled design on your sheet of watercolor paper (instructions on pages 48–49).

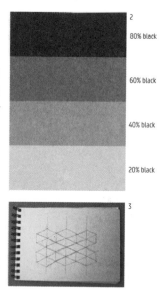

2

80% black

60% black

40% black

20% black

3

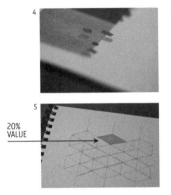

4

5

20%
VALUE

④ Mix a hue—any hue—with a value that matches the 20% bar on your printed value strip. Check your color's value by painting a small swatch of it onto the 20% bar of the value strip and letting it dry (gouache tends to darken slightly as it dries and acrylics usually dry without a change in value). Next, squint your eyes at the painted swatch. Squint so hard you can barely see the swatch: It's at this point where your eyes will be less influenced by the swatch's color and more able to compare the color's value with its 20% gray backdrop. ⑤ Add white to the color if its value is too light and add black (or a dark color) if the hue needs to be darkened. When your color's value matches the 20% gray, use it to paint the top center diamond of your design.

⑥ Mix another hue. Aim for a 40% value with this color and formulate the hue so that it pairs nicely with your first color. Fill the space indicated here with the color. Your design's first painted form is beginning to take shape. ⑦ Fill the next panel of the design with a color that has a value of 60%, and again, mix this color so that it looks good next to the previously painted hues.

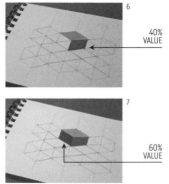

6

40%
VALUE

7

60%
VALUE

More cubes will be painted in the steps ahead: If the values in each cube are on target then each will have a convincing dimensional appearance. Furthermore, if you get the values right, then you can fully enjoy the freedom of being able to choose hues and levels of saturation that please your eye.

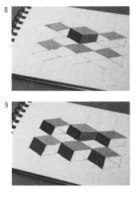

⑧ Fill in the rest of your cubes' upper spaces with a variety of colors that are each 20% in value.

⑨ Add colors with a 60% value to the cubes' darker sides. Tips: Use black, grays, browns or darker colors to deepen a hue's value and add a color's complement if you want to reduce its saturation.

Don't worry too much about painting perfectly shaped forms for this exercise: Aim instead for a consistent level of neatness—however neat or un-neat that may be.

*A reminder: The main reason this book's images are in black and white is so that you will not be influenced by their colors. Use colors that appeal to **you** for this book's exercises!*

⑩ Fill the remainder of the cubes' panels with a variety of hues that are 40% in value. Sit back from time to time as you work and squint your eyes to evaluate the consistency of the values used throughout the design: Look for panels that appear either too dark or too light and make adjustments as needed. ⑪ Finish your colorful geometrical design by filling its background with a color (bright or muted) that has a value of 80%.

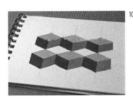

10

11

After completing this project, did you notice how you not only gained insights into values, but also into the moods and the ways of water, paint and brushes? Good stuff to know—all of it.

Design-drawing instructions. Follow these steps to create the foundational drawing used for this activity's painting. Briefly practice these steps, if you like, on a scrap piece of paper before committing pencil to watercolor paper.

Pencil a vertical line down the center of the page. Add a widely proportioned X to the center of the line.

Add an X above the first one you drew, and then add another below. (All freshly drawn lines are shown in black in this and the following diagrams.)

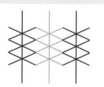

Repeat your current design two more times: one on either side of the original. Note that the lines of the previously drawn Xs can be extended to form the lines of the Xs in the design's new portions.

 Cap the top and bottom Xs with angled lines like so.

 Draw eight vertical lines to define the edges of the cubes that you will be painting in this exercise.

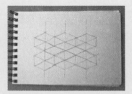 Your finished drawing should look similar to this. Since the paint used for this project will be opaque, and since the design will be filled in with paint, little or no evidence of your penciled lines will remain once the project is complete.

Activity
#6

CATEGORY:
INK AND PAINT

JUNK DRAWER PRINTMAKING. Most of us, somewhere in our homes, have a drawer, box or bin full of buttons, spools of thread, retired household items and a collection of keys that may or may not be associated with any current locks. Chances are, these items will someday make their way to recycling bins or to garbage cans, but before they do, how about giving them the chance to leave one last impression—both figuratively and literally? How about creating a set of frame-ready pieces of art using some of these objects as printmaking tools?

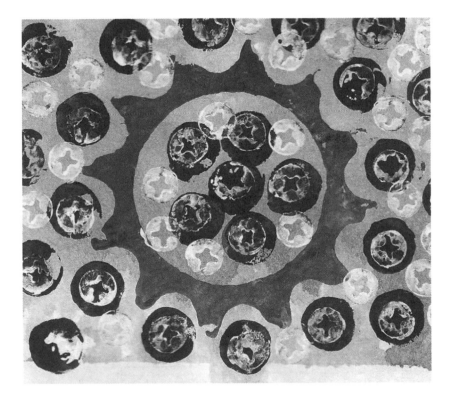

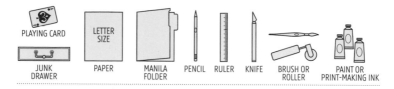

PLAYING CARD
JUNK DRAWER
PAPER
LETTER SIZE
MANILA FOLDER
PENCIL
RULER
KNIFE
BRUSH OR ROLLER
PAINT OR PRINT-MAKING INK

Activity 6: Junk drawer printmaking. Gather a good assortment of junk drawer items for this project—things that you won't mind covering with a bit of paint or ink. Printmaking ink would be ideal for this activity, but acrylics, gouache or watercolors could be used instead. Protect your work surface with newsprint or butcher paper.

① Gather your assortment of junk and semi-useless items. ② To prepare for the upcoming works of art, cut a playing-card-sized hole in your manila folder as shown here (trace the playing card to define the size and shape of the hole). It's not critical that the hole be placed in the exact center of the folder's panel—what is being made here is a simple mask through which paint can be applied.

③ Cut a playing-card-sized hole in the folder's other panel and then cut the folder in two.

④ Next, fold five or six sheets of paper in half.

⑤ Position one of your manila folder masks over a half-sheet of paper (each print that will be made in the steps ahead will occupy a half-sheet). In a moment we'll be applying a light wash of color into this mask—a subtle backdrop for the upcoming printed impressions.

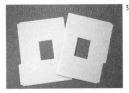

This exercise is a little more involved—and will take a little more time—than most of the projects in this book. Stick with it: The results should justify the extra effort and will likely result in an attractive set of ready-for-display prints.

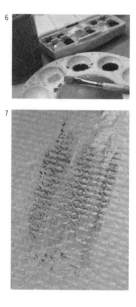

⑥ Whether you're using printmaking ink, watercolors, gouache or acrylics, mix a light, semi-watery puddle of color. A pale neutral tone such as a beige or a warm gray would work perfectly, but as long as the color is light, any hue will do.
⑦ Now, instead of brushing the color directly through the mask and onto the paper, apply it to something like a small sheet of paper, a crumpled piece of foil or a padded plastic envelope (as shown here). Apply the paint to an area that is slightly larger than the size of the cut-out mask that was created earlier.

⑧ Next, press your freshly painted surface into the masked area of your half-sheet of paper and then remove it to leave a mottled wash of color inside the mask. ⑨ Remove the mask from the page and repeat what you just did to the other half of the sheet of paper. This will leave you with two lightly and irregularly colored backdrops. Produce at least ten backdrops in this way so that you'll have plenty to work with when you start adding printed impressions in the next step. Allow all of your backdrops to dry before proceeding.

No time to wait? Use a hair dryer to speed the drying process of your backdrop panels.

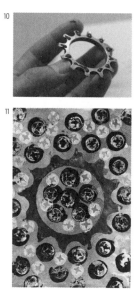

⑩ Ready to start printing? Choose something from your pile of objects, mix a color of ink or paint, apply the color to the object and then stamp it into one of your prepared backdrops. Some objects will accept ink or paint more readily than others, but don't worry too much about this: Go with the flow and make an impression of the object (possibly on a spare sheet of paper) and see what happens. Experiment with different pigment-and-water ratios to find out what works and what doesn't. ⑪ Build up layers of various-colored stamped images within your backdrops. Think: color, composition, balance, flow. This pattern was made from a bicycle cog, a round piece of plastic and the head of a screw.

(12) As an option, what about working with printmaking ink and a small roller? Here, printmaking ink is being applied to a roller using a small piece of glass as a rolling surface.

(13) Once the roller has been coated with a thin layer of ink, the pigment can by rolled onto an object (such as this round metal socket) prior to using the object as a stamp.

(14) If you have access to printmaking ink and a small roller, you may find that this method works very well in capturing small details of whatever it is you are using to create stamped images. The image shown here—a design built by stamping impressions of four different keys—was created using printmaking ink and a roller.

A small gallery of prints made from the junk drawer contents seen on page 52 are featured here. Are you happy with your stamped creations? What about framing a few and putting them on display (as seen on page 67, for instance)? How about scanning your prints and presenting them digitally as a screen-saving slideshow on your computer?

Even if you decide not to showcase your prints, consider saving them for possible use in future professional or personal projects. Who knows, one might make the perfect piece of featured art or backdrop material for a client's brochure, annual report or advertisement. Also, keep in mind that the stamping technique demonstrated here could be used to create a custom piece of art for a client—artwork built using the client's products or tools-of-the-trade as printmaking stamps.

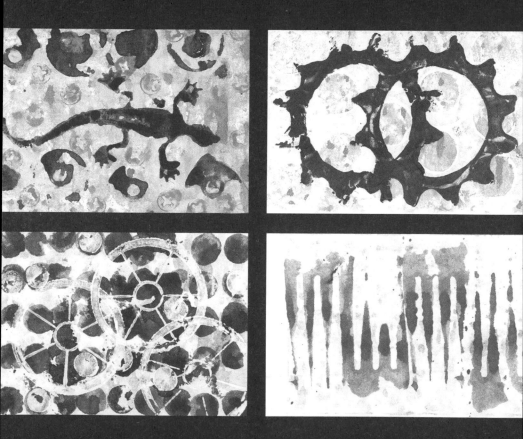

Activity
#

CATEGORY:
COMPOSITION

NOODLE DOODLES. You've probably heard of the value of including elements of fun and familiarity in art lessons aimed at a child, but have you ever wondered how well these teaching tactics work when directed at a grown-up? A grown-up like you? Here's your chance to find out by employing the ever-popular grade-school media of pasta and glue to explore and enforce layout-related lessons of composition and conveyance. This project is as likely as any in *D30* to produce presentable pieces of art. Got room on a wall in your kitchen for a few framed noodle doodles?

| LETTER SIZE |
| PAPER | GLUE | PASTA | TWEEZERS | TIME NEEDED: ABOUT AN HOUR |

Activity 7: Noodle doodles. Everything you'll need for this project can probably be found in your home or at a grocery store: an assortment of pastas (such as those featured at right), a few sheets of letter-size paper and some ordinary white glue. Tweezers might come in handy, too, when it comes to gluing your pasta to paper in *just* the right places.

① Take a couple pieces of letter-size paper and fold them into quarters. Next, cut the sheets along the folds. Each of your upcoming creations will be made on one of the resulting quarter-sheets.

Many of this book's exercises fit on pieces of paper of this size. Why? It's to improve the chances that the various works of art you create will look good when presented as a set. (Page 67 offers a look at a framed set of this kind.)

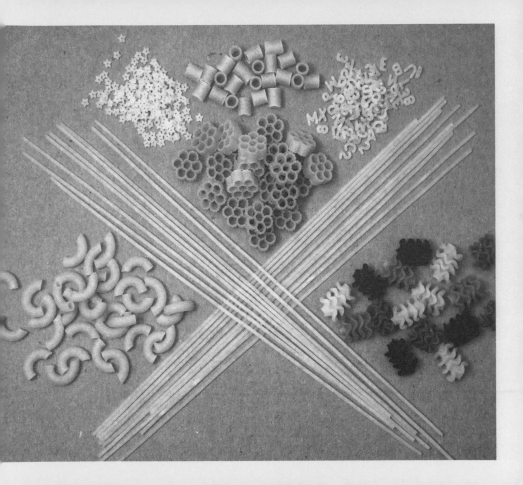

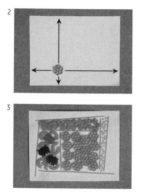

2

3

② This is a warm-up, so don't bother gluing your pasta to the paper. Select a noodle and place it on one of your quarter-size pieces of paper, but don't just place it anywhere: Aim for a spot where the distances above, below and to either side of the noodle are each different. Why look for this kind of placement? Because it's a surefire way of generating visual interest: *Unequal spaces lend conveyances of action and movement to compositions.* Keep this axiom in mind when constructing most of this activity's designs.

③ Unequal spacing can be applied to divisions of space, too: Use noodles and glue to create a design that features divisions of space that are of different sizes and various proportions.

④ Use pasta and glue to build several more designs. Pay particular attention to unequal spacing as you work, and make a point of coming up with completely different solutions for each of your creations. ⑤ Apply the theme of "grouping" to at least one composition: a design that features several groups of different sizes and differing characteristics. ⑥ In this sample, a neatly flowing ribbon of pasta flowers has been laid on top of a contrasting backdrop of randomly placed macaronies. Create one or more designs that deliver the contradictory conveyances of harmony and contrast, rhythm and randomness.

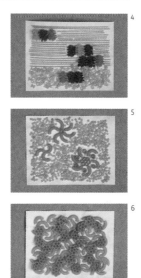

4

5

6

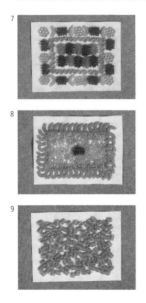

⑦+⑧ The first of the tightly structured designs at left has no clear center of interest. The second has a very distinct focal point. Craft a pair of compositions: one with and one without a strong center of interest. Consider setting aside the axiom of unequal spacing for these creations and aim instead for a static placement of elements.

⑨ Release your grip on any notions of control as you wrap up this activity: Let the noodles fall where they will as you produce one or two wholly random assemblages—expressionistic abstractions conveyed through the media of pasta and glue.

Many of this book's art projects are designed to fit on similarly sized pieces of paper to improve the chances that they will look good when hung as sets on the walls of your home, cubicle or office. Here, the products of four of this book's exercises have been placed on top of deeply embossed sheets of metallic paper and placed inside ornate metal frames.

Activity
8
CATEGORY:
WRITING

HAIKU, FOR YOU. Creative cross-training: That's what this exercise is really about. This project—which will occupy as little or as much time as you can devote to it over the next seven days—is designed to give you the chance to set aside your normal image-based creative output in favor of a different medium: words. And if the idea of squeezing seven writing exercises into your already packed daily routine seems daunting, don't fret: The haiku poems you'll be composing during this week's coffee breaks and bus rides only need to contain a handful of words and just seventeen syllables.

HAIKU TO A PARTICULAR MORNING

Coffee, laptop? Check.
Earphones, glasses, headache? Check.
Monday morning? Check.

NOTEBOOK   PEN   THESAURUS

Activity 8: Haiku, for you. Try leaving your computer out of this exercise and using only old-school writing tools such as pen and paper. Beyond that, not much is needed other than a few minutes from each of the next seven days that can be devoted to thoughtful observation, creative writing and the counting of syllables.

Haiku poems are a brief set of verses that typically evoke impressions of nature and of human experiences. Traditional haikus tend to deal with the natural world and its seasons, but there is no mandate for this. Haiku poetry often connects with readers through "aha" moments where the reader feels a beyond-words affinity with the scene, event, experience or sensation being described.

The quiet pond
A frog leaps in
The sound of the water
BASHO (1644–1694)

TIME NEEDED:
ABOUT AN HOUR

In terms of structure, haiku poems take several forms. Here we'll be dealing with the most common and traditional form, where the poem consists of seventeen syllables written in three lines: the poem's top and bottom lines contain five syllables each and its middle line contains seven syllables.*

*Most well-known examples of traditional Japanese haikus (such as the three examples in the outer columns of this spread) do not seem to adhere to the seventeen-syllable definition of a haiku poem. Keep in mind, however, that in their original language, they were written to follow this structure—a structure that was lost when the words were translated to English.

Don't swat that fly
It wrings its hands
It wrings its feet
ISSA (1763–1827)

Over the wintry
Forest, winds howl in rage
With no leaves to blow
SOSEKI (1275–1351)

SATURDAY NIGHT
Better judgment and
The green margarita drained
It's Dairy Queen next.

BELIZE
Music quits, bus halts
Driver probes CD player
With guard's machete

Featured here are two contemporary examples of haiku poetry (contemporary in that one is intentionally silly and the other involves a specific observation of a present-day scene and situation). Though modern in their content, both of these haikus follow the traditional three line 5–7–5 syllable format. The haiku poems you'll be creating will also adhere to this structure.

Haiku is full of contradictions: It's serious except when it's silly and its messages are obscure except when they are crystal clear. Creative wiggle-room like this makes haiku a fun—and low pressure—undertaking for people who are new to expressive forms of writing.

It's time to write. Got a pen? A piece of paper? A thesaurus (electronic or paper)? Good. You're ready to go.

Brainstorm for subject matter but don't overthink it: The best haikus often deal with the most everyday occurrences. Some ideas: a daily routine, a daily treat, the personality of a friend, a behavior or the appearance of a pet, a favorite food or beverage, the time of the year, the day of the week, today's weather, yesterday's news.

Next, start writing down thoughts, details, descriptors, impressions and actions related to the subject. Don't worry about constructing the haiku yet: Just jot down things that come to mind when you think of your subject.

After you've brainstormed your subject for a while and have a good feel for what it is you'll be trying to convey through your haiku, start penning lines and counting syllables. Be open-minded and tenacious as you work. Keep looking for just the right way to construct your verses so that they end up in a 5–7–5 syllable format. Use a thesaurus to help find words with just the right syllable count, and be open to shifting the way your message is assembled and delivered in order to get everything just right. When you come up with a completed haiku, give yourself a quick pat on the back and then try out alternative versions of the poem—versions that might well turn out to be improvements on what you originally thought was your best effort.

The final piece of this project is this: Write another haiku tomorrow. Write about anything. Write during a coffee break, on the bus ride home from work, after dinner or before bed. Whatever works for you. How about making it a goal to write seven haikus in the next seven days?

How about keeping a journal of favorite personal haikus? What about making a piece of art that combines one of your paintings or photos with the words of one of your haiku poems? How about handcrafting a small book that features your haikus—handwritten or typographically printed—on the left-hand pages, and your artwork and/or photos on the right-hand pages?

Peter Piper picked
A peck of pickled peppers
Hey, this is haiku

Activity # 9

CATEGORY:
VIDEO

THINKING IN EDITS. The bad guy's sedan races across the movie screen and a split second later a police car zooms past with lights flashing. Now the bad guy—his forehead perspiring—is glancing between the road and his cracked rearview mirror as he cuts through traffic. Next, we see the cop car's shaky image in the cracked mirror, followed by a building-top perspective of both cars threading their way through crowded downtown streets. The policeman's perspective is next on the screen as we watch his white-knuckled hands grip the steering wheel while the suspect's car careens around a corner just ahead. Welcome to the movies. Welcome to the magic of editing.

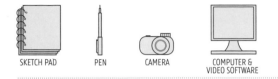

SKETCH PAD PEN CAMERA COMPUTER & VIDEO SOFTWARE

Activity 9: Thinking in edits. A smartphone or a pocket digital camera that can record videos will be fine for this project. A camcorder or a DSLR would be good, too, but neither of these high-quality options are in any way mandatory. A computer and basic video editing software will be needed to assemble quick clips of footage into a short video.

Begin this project by imagining how the scene described perviously might have been recorded if the film crew were limited to just one camera. Really think about this: Until the recent proliferation of small, low cost, high resolution digital cameras, the scene would have likely been filmed by a crew who placed their one-and-only camera in various positions and then filmed the scene (or portions of the scene) multiple times. Afterward, an editor would have connected the various clips of footage into a captivating—and chronological—action sequence.

Ready for a home-brewed, low-fi editing activity of your own? This project should, at the very least, boost your appreciation and awareness of the efforts

TIME NEEDED:
A COUPLE HOURS OR MORE

that filmmakers go through to create multi-point-of-view scenes*—efforts and cinematic techniques you may have been taking for granted.

Your challenge here will to be to create an ultra-short movie (a minute or two would be fine) from a series of very short scenes. For example, a mini movie about a dog fetching a ball could be created by filming individual scenes of the following: the dog laying on the floor, a hand picking up a ball, the dog's ears perking and its head lifting, the ball being thrown, the dog leaping into action and out of the frame, the ball skimming along the ground, the dog running and leaping over obstacles, onlookers turning their heads as if watching the dog, the dog snatching the ball from the ground, close ups of a wagging tail and the dog chewing contentedly on the ball. (Keep in mind that these scenes could be shot in any order, and then be assembled into their desired chronological appearance using video editing software).

Brainstorm ideas for your own mini movie. Something as simple as a game of fetch, making and flipping pancakes, or changing a lightbulb would be perfect. Briefly plan your scenes by making a thumbnail sketch of what each will include (a process known as a storyboarding).

Be creative and resourceful as you shoot each of your scenes. Don't just aim the camera and pull the trigger: Compose each scene as creatively and attractively as you can. If you don't like a particular "take," rerecord it.

 Use basic movie editing software to assemble your scenes into a continuous sequence (your recently-purchased computer or camera may have come with this kind of software; free and low-cost video software can be found online). Experiment as you edit and compose your clips into a continuous piece: Remove excess footage from your clips, see how short you can make each clip while still conveying a cohesive storyline, try tinting or otherwise treating your footage with visual effects offered through your video software. Turn your creation into a web-worthy film by adding music, a title and credits. Prepare to be amazed at how your short

bits of disconnected footage have been converted into a self-contained, story-telling and entertaining mini movie using your camera and software.

An interesting footnote to the topic of multi-POV editing is that it wasn't until several years after the invention of motion pictures that it was determined that yes, audiences would clearly understand the on-screen sequence of events if, for instance, footage of a fireman raising a ladder to an upper-floor window of a burning building was followed by an interior view of a fireman coming in through a broken window to rescue one of the building's occupants. These days, of course, filmmakers don't think twice about presenting scenes from multiple perspectives, and few viewers are even aware of the detailed planning and the feats of cinematic ingenuity that go into creating these scenes—whether they are of a family talking across the dinner table or a high speed car chase through downtown traffic.

Why create videos if you are not a videographer? It's because there's no artistic workout that will exercise half as many creative muscles as that of planning, filming and editing a comprehensive video project. If you are new to videography, here's a tip: Don't worry too much about the things you don't know and the equipment you don't own—simply make the most of

your current skillset and your current array of equipment and make videos that you will enjoy watching. Over time, and after a few video projects, you'll likely find that your skills involving photography, composition, movement, music, storytelling, color, typography, computers, cameras and software will have improved significantly (along with your desire to begin your next video project).

Activity
10
CATEGORY:
TYPOGRAPHY

CHARACTER STUDY. Considering the almost supernatural aesthetic perfection of the world's great typefaces, it almost seems a shame they are so commonly used to form words, thoughts and ideas that are consumed, processed—and mostly forgotten—almost as soon as the eye passes over them. Let's stop, then, and take the time to see, appreciate and learn from a few gorgeously crafted typographic specimens. And what better way to do this than by creating portraits that allow us to follow—with utmost care and attention—their every stroke, curve, bend and arc with our eyes, our pens and our paintbrushes?

PAPER   PENCIL   PEN   YOUR CHOICE OF ART MEDIA

Activity 10: Character study. Pencil, pen and paper will be used for this activity, as well as any other media that suits your fancy, including colored pencils, chalks, charcoals, crayons, watercolors, acrylics, inks, clays, needle and thread, paper mache, stencils, art papers, origami papers, collage material, glitter and glue.

① Begin by doing a blind contour drawing of the ampersand on page 90. What's a blind contour drawing? It's where you put pen to paper and follow the exterior of what you see with your eyes and a pen—without ever once peeking at what you are drawing until you are finished. Don't worry about the appearance of your drawing: Simply enjoy the experience of letting your eyes look very closely at a subject and your hand the opportunity to become better linked with what your eyes see.

② Move on to another quick drawing exercise that will boost your brain's connection with—and its appreciation of—exquisite typographic forms. Get a pencil and a piece of paper and turn to the pair of numerals on page 91. Next, draw the numbers without actually drawing the numbers: That is, draw the spaces *between and inside* their forms. Focusing on the negative spaces within and around the numerals will encourage your brain to comprehend the characters' lines, curves and shapes instead of working toward a rendering of what it *thinks* the numbers ought to look like. This kind of perception-boosting exercise can also be applied to dimensional objects: See the exercise on page 158, Positively Negative, for more about drawing negative spaces.

Complete this exercise by creating a portrait of a letter. Choose whatever character—in whatever typeface—you like. Print a large sample of the letter on a sheet of paper that can be used for reference as you work (or use one of the already enlarged specimens on the next spread as your subject). Render the portrait using your media of choice, and portray the character's form as accurately as you can, no matter what media you use. (Full artistic freedom can enter the equation when you get around to filling the space around your featured character.) The image above, as well as the one on page 85, are just a couple examples of the kinds of portraits being described here: Take your own creation in whatever thematic and visual directions seem most fitting to you.

Ideas: The next time you need a drop-cap* for a design project, consider rendering the letter using pencil, paint or ink; use a hand-rendered letter or numeral as an illustration for an article, a brochure or a poster; create a drawing of a friend's initials, frame the artwork and give it as a gift; design and create a custom-rendered monogram for use as a personal logo.

* Drop-caps are the large letters sometimes used at the beginning of paragraphs. See page 116 for an example of a drop-cap in action.

GOUDY OLD STYLE ITALIC

BODONI POSTER

HELVETICA

REQUIEM TEXT ROMAN

Activity
#**11**
CATEGORY:
DIMENSIONAL

SHRINE ON A SHELF. The art that most graphic designers create is tailored according to the demands of clients and the clock, and the great majority of that art is produced using the computer and other digital tools. And while there's nothing wrong with digitally creating art in a timely manner in exchange for a paycheck, it's a routine that often runs contrary to most artists' yearning for creative outlets that are not dependant on clients, schedules or electricity. Here, then, is a project that's about as free-ranging and non-digital as they get: just what the doctor ordered for the modern designer in need of some unbounded, unjudged and unplugged artistic expression.

Activity 11: Shrine on a shelf. Got a few—or a bunch—of keepsake items floating around your home or office? Travel souvenirs, letters, cards or craft projects? Interesting bottles, shells, game pieces or well-used childrens' toys? How about looking through drawers, closets, the attic and your basement to come up with a cache of these kinds of things for this activity?

(BEFORE)

① The plan here is simple: Search for and collect items of the above-mentioned variety and arrange them in a shrine-like way on a shelf, a countertop or anywhere else where you can let the assemblage remain for enjoyment and contemplation (as well as for future additions and revisions). Arrange your objects in a compositionally compelling way as you mindfully aim for conveyances of passion, whimsy, nostalgia or whatever else suits your fancy: *You* are both client and creator for this project.

(AFTER)

② Got space on a bookshelf that you can allocate to a shrine built from personally precious material? ③ Attend to details both large and small. A miniature sand garden sits at the base of this assemblage. Laying in the quarter-inch-thick bed of fine sand are a variety of beads, stones, marbles, jacks, dried plants and other miscellaneous items that contribute to the shrine's visual intrigue and its thematic conveyances.

At right, more examples of at-home shrines devoted to the themes of Italian espresso and precious junk. (A painted spice shelf found at a garage sale was used for the espresso shrine.)

Activity
#**12**
CATEGORY:
PHOTOGRAPHY

MIRROR IMAGES. Most designers spend a fair amount of time *working* in Photoshop, but not a lot of time *playing* with this versatile image-manipulation program. In this exercise, you'll be given the chance to do just that: *play*. The guidelines here are simple and mainly involve choosing photographs from your hard drive and converting them into an intriguing set of kaleidoscopic images using basic transformation techniques. Feel free to take things further using additional techniques and digital tools if you feel so inclined.

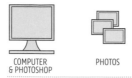

COMPUTER
& PHOTOSHOP

PHOTOS

Activity 12: Mirror images. Not much is needed for this project—just a computer loaded with Photoshop and some photos from your image cache (you may also shoot new photos for this exercise, if you prefer). Any type of image will work, but once you dive into this exercise, you'll soon discover which kinds of photos produce the results that impress you most.

① Images with clear and strongly composed content make ideal subjects for this exercise. Select at least a half-dozen such photos from your hard drive. Open the images in Photoshop and maximize their appearance with basic color and contrast adjustments (if necessary) before moving ahead.

Basic Photoshop know-how is needed for this project. If you are new to Photoshop, consult the program's Help *menu as needed.*

TIME NEEDED:
ABOUT AN HOUR

② Open your image document in Photoshop
and double its size both horizontally and vertically
(use the *Image > Canvas Size* menu to do this).
Keep the original image in the upper left corner
of the document and copy it as shown here.
③ Afterward, your document's images should
be arranged like so. Each of the four images
should be on a separate layer and there should
be no space between the copies. ④ Now you're
ready to create a kaleidoscopic design from
the four images: Flip the upper right image
horizontally, the lower left image vertically,
and the lower right image both horizontally
and vertically (use the *Edit > Transform* menu
to accomplish these tasks).

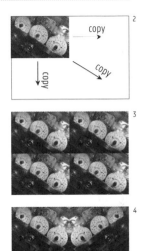

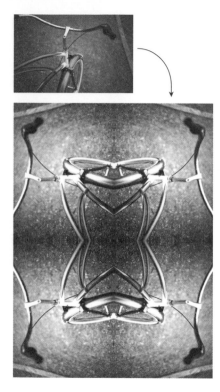

The kaleidoscopic treatment described on the previous page has been applied to the three photographs featured along the top of this spread. Ready to try this on your own? Treat at least six photos to this effect: Images of this kind look especially good when presented as a set.

Would your image look better in color or in black and white? Should your photo be cropped prior to treating it to this effect? Would digital enhancements or special effects further improve the look of your kaleidoscopic creation? Consider your options and go with what you like best.

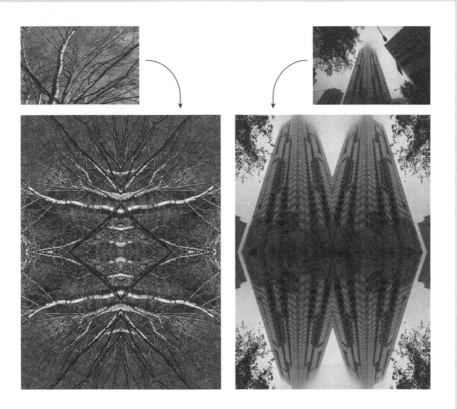

Be sure to explore variations of the kaleidoscopic theme presented in this section. Here, for instance, a flower borrowed from the Instant Photo Studio activity on page 210 has been removed from its backdrop, copied and rotated to form an intricate spiraling design. An image like this has real potential for both personal and professional projects: Spend time learning how to make the most of Photoshop's image transformation tools.

IN THE STYLE OF. We seem to spend more than enough time in our own heads, so how about spending an hour or so in someone else's? In fact, what about making ourselves at home in the head of a famous writer with a penetrating and no-nonsense view of people and life? Afterward, when we return entirely to our own heads, we will likely bring with us an expanded perception of the human experience, along with an improved ability to communicate our perceptions—a capacity that is bound to have a positive influence on all our creative output.

It was a summer of wistaria. The twilight was full of it and of the smell of his father's cigar as they sat on the front gallery after supper until it would be time for Quentin to start, while in the deep shaggy lawn below the veranda the fireflies blew and drifted in soft random—the odor, the scent, which five months later Mr. Compson's letter would carry up from Mississippi and over the long iron New England snow and into Quentin's sitting-room at Harvard.

PAPER   WRITING TOOL OF CHOICE

Activity 13: In the style of. Use a pen, pencil, computer or typewriter for this writing project—whatever allows you to work most efficiently and to think most expansively. It's difficult to say for sure how much time you'll need for this exercise since writing skills—and writing speeds—vary greatly. How about giving it at least an hour? More, if you like.

Take a look at the two-sentence excerpt on the previous page. It's the opening paragraph from William Faulkner's novel, *Absalom, Absalom!* The clipping's first sentence is brief, concise and descriptive. The second is long, meandering, grammatically challenging, difficult to follow *and* spectacularly descriptive. The text pretty much insists on (and is entirely worthy of) multiple readings—readings that gradually divulge multi-layered conveyances and impressions that may end up feeling more like the reader's own recollections than like fictional occurrences in the lives of made-up characters.

TIME NEEDED:
ABOUT AN HOUR

The upcoming exercise will involve writing a few lines of your own in the story-telling voice of William Faulker. Mr. Faulker's writing will be an ideal model for this exercise since his prose seems bound by few technical or stylistic restrictions (good news for those of us who are not seasoned novelists, right?) while also being a ringing example of observational acuity and root-level integrity.

Interviewer: *What technique do you use to arrive at your standard?*
Faulkner: *Let the writer take up surgery or brick-laying if he is interested in technique. There is no mechanical way to get the writing done, no shortcut. The young writer would be a fool to follow a theory. Teach yourself by your own mistakes; people learn only by error.* FROM AN INTERVIEW PUBLISHED IN **THE PARIS REVIEW**, 1956

Ready to compose? The upcoming challenge will involve writing a paragraph that is about the same length as Faulkner's sample on page 107. Additionally, your paragraph should be similar Faulkner's in that it should contain two sentences: One that is short and concise and one that is lengthy, wandering, grammatically debatable and piercingly descriptive.

In terms of subject matter, choose something connected with a familiar place, event or routine. For example, you could write about the process of brewing coffee or tea, your morning or evening commute, an aspect of a favorite sporting activity or the experience of a walk around the block or a hike through nature. Anything. Look around you now. What comes to mind? Don't give yourself more than a minute or two to choose a subject—just choose something and prepare to reach deeply for its most truthful and telling conveyances.

Begin by mentally surveying the sensations, emotions, sights, actions, sounds, and smells connected with your subject. Spend several minutes taking notes on this material before you start drafting your paragraph in earnest.

Use your first sentence to set the stage for your written piece and all that it is meant to convey. Use matter-of-fact language for this sentence—language that will contrast nicely with the flowing, descriptive and decidedly *not* matter-of-fact wording of the very long sentence that will follow.

Choose only the most compelling material from your notes as you stitch together your paragraph's much longer—and much more evocative—second sentence. Continually listen to the sound, the rhythm and the flow of this sentence's words as it builds toward the whole of what it intends to convey and communicate.

Be patient and methodical as you work. Take to heart the words of advice (and encouragement) that another much-read and much-admired novelist once wrote about the process of writing:

It is a lot like inflating a blimp with a bicycle pump. Anybody can do it. All it takes is time. KURT VONNEGUT

If you start to feel discouraged as you work on your paragraph, stop (stop feeling discouraged, that is, but keep on writing) and remember: This project is not for a client, not for review and not for publication. This project is for you. This project is for the experience of looking deeply into a real-life experience and finding out how it feels to describe that experience through an intriguing and  compelling assemblage of words.

When, at last, you are reasonably satisfied with your paragraph, set it aside. You are done for now.

Tomorrow, or the next day, look at it again. (It's rare when a writer doesn't find things they'd like to change when they look at a piece of writing with fresh eyes.) Make adjustments as you see fit and once again set your piece aside for a day or two.

Finish your piece the next time you take it out for review and refinement.

Read, read, read. Read everything—trash, classics, good and bad, and see how they do it. Just like a carpenter who works as an apprentice and studies the master. **Read!** You'll absorb it. Then write. If it is good, you'll find out. If it's not, throw it out the window. WILLIAM FAULKNER

MAKE A FACE. Get your camera and some props: It's time to photograph faces. And we're not talking people portraits here—this time the faces are going to be of the typographic variety, and we'll be using special arrangements of our props as subject matter. The best part of this exercise is that it will enforce a collection of positive lessons pertaining to typography, composition, photography *and* resourcefulness. The next best thing is that the exercise will leave you with a custom-built ready-to-go assortment of characters that could be used for both personal and professional art and design projects.

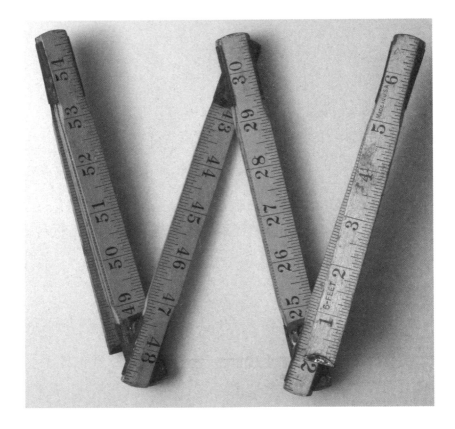

CAMERA

COMPUTER
& PHOTOSHOP

TIME NEEDED:
ABOUT AN HOUR

Activity 14: Make a face. Here, we'll be making letters from *things*. Good sources of *things* include kitchen drawers, clothes closets, jewelry chests, craft supply boxes, sewing kits, hardware stashes, office supply caches and garage shelves. As far as a camera goes, use the best camera you have—whether that's a smartphone camera, a pocket camera or a DSLR.

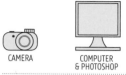

re you at home? At the office? Perfect. Chances are, everything you'll need for this project is on hand. The instructions for this activity are simple: Build a letter of the alphabet (uppercase, lowercase or both) using material from sources like those listed above. Snap a picture of the letter (photo tips are on the next spread) and then clear your workspace and start on another character. Create an entire alphabet this way. Use the same material for each letter or build each from something different: It's entirely up to you. Consider your options, gather building material for a few minutes and then get started.

othing special was used to photograph the hand-built characters shown here. A bright desk lamp was used to illuminate the letters (each of which was assembled on top of a white piece of paper) and a pocket digital camera was used to shoot the photos. Each of these images was photographed from directly above, but you could explore other perspectives if you like. The alphabet shown here was photographed in color and then converted to black and white in Photoshop: Your own alphabet could be finalized similarly or it could be presented in color. What about using something other than a white backdrop for your creations? How about applying digital treatments to your images? The options are many: Aim for outcomes you love.

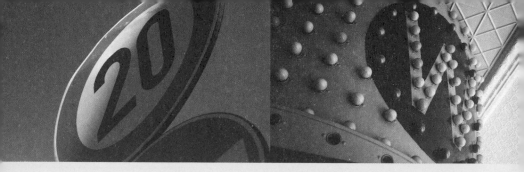

What about building a complete photographic alphabet from real-life letters and numbers? A project like this could be started and finished in a single afternoon, or it could be carried out over an extended period of time. One good thing about making this a longer-range project is that it would provide you with extra incentive to exercise two extremely beneficial creative habits: keeping a pocket digital camera with you at all times and keeping your eyes open for photo opportunities. Images such as these could come in handy for all kinds of personal and professional projects and they would also make a nice-looking display on their own.

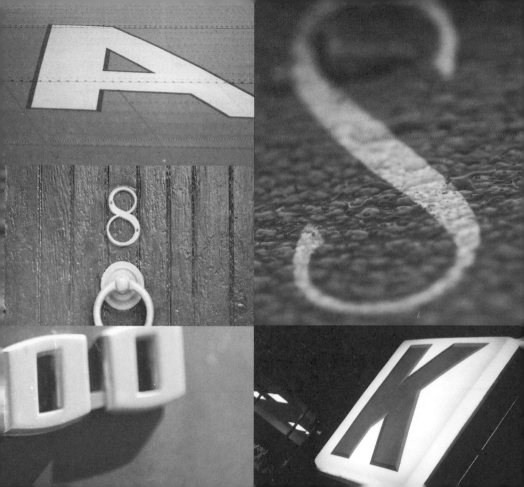

HARMONY AND CONTRAST. Split-complementary palettes feature a color plus the two hues on either side of the color's complement. Many designers are especially fond of these palettes since split complements are able to deliver a sophisticated mix of conveyances: Harmony is derived from the close association between a color's near-complementary hues, contrast emerges from the solo hue on the opposite side of the color wheel, and endless variety can be explored by varying the values and saturation (defined on page 41) of each of the palette's colors. Create and apply your own split-complementary palettes in this simple and fun watercolor project.

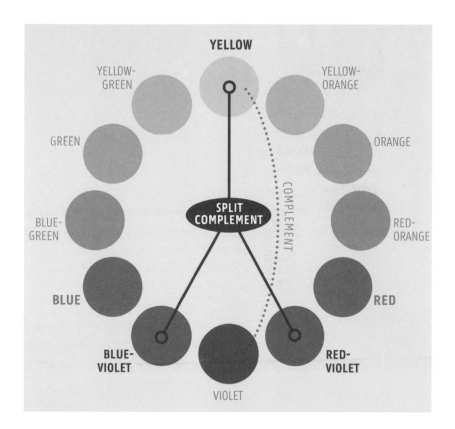

WATERCOLOR PAD | PENCIL | BRUSH | WATERCOLORS | PAINT MIXING TRAY | WATER JAR | RAG OR PAPER TOWEL

Activity 15: Harmony and contrast. Anything from high-quality tubes of watercolors to student-grade watercolor kits will work here. You'll also need a small pad or piece of watercolor paper, a pencil, a fine-tipped brush (a #2 watercolor brush was used for this project's samples), a paint-mixing tray, a jar of water and a rag for clean up.

① Collect your supplies and find a well-lit place to work. A plastic or ceramic paint mixing tray like the one shown here would work nicely as a mixing station for your paints, as would the partitioned lid of a metal or plastic watercolor tray.

Take another look at the previous spread if you are unsure about how split-complementary sets of colors are found: You will creating these palettes with your paints beginning in step 4.

TIME NEEDED:
AN HOUR OR TWO

② Prepare your piece of watercolor paper by penciling this design. Create the design's five circles by tracing a coin—a quarter was used here.
③ Next, loosely draw a square around each circle (the corners of the squares may touch, but they don't have to) and then draw a small square inside each circle.

Watercolors soak into paper; penciled lines do not. Because of this, you will be able to erase your guidelines once all your paint has dried (unless you'd rather leave them, that is—the choice is yours).

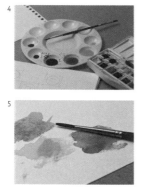

④+⑤ Begin by making a small puddle of likeable color and testing its appearance on a piece of scrap paper. After that, mentally locate your color's complement on the color wheel and create two more puddles of color: one for each of the hues on either side of your first color's complement (and again, see pages 122–123 if you need a reminder of how split-complementary palettes can be found). You should now have three ready-to-go colors.

Don't worry about scientific accuracy as you create your split complementary palette: Just use your best judgement and adjust the hue, saturation and value (defined on page 41) of each of the colors until you are happy with the way they look as a set.

⑥ Apply a watery covering of your three colors to the design's central circle/square element (it's up to you which color goes where) *and leave a thin gap of dry white paper between each of the colors.* ⑦ Next, while the paint is still wet, use the tip of your brush to create a few tiny connections across the dry white gaps to invite small areas of color to mix and blend in watery and semi-controlled ways. ⑧ Finish by applying a different trio of split complementary colors to each of your circle/square elements in the same manner. Aim for an attractive range of hues, values and levels of saturation throughout the design, and be sure to carry what you've learned here about split-complementary palettes into future creative projects of your own.

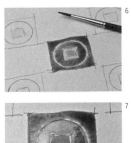

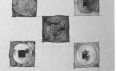

Conversation with self, part ii.

If you have completed anywhere near half of this book's
activities (either in order or randomly), then now is a good
time to stop and answer a few questions in this pen-and-
paper brainstorming session. The questions ahead are
designed to help solidify significant insights, ideas and
goals that may have propped up while you worked on the
previous activities. Not only that, they should also assist
in generating new mental matter that will connect with
the impulses and ideals that come to mind as you work
through the book's remaining projects.

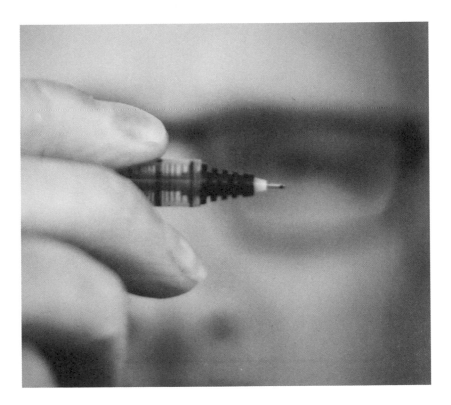

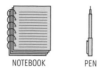

NOTEBOOK   PEN

Activity 16: Conversation with self, part II. Turn off the television, shut down the computer, grab a pen and a notebook, find a comfortable place to work, take a couple deep breaths, clear your head and commit to spending the next hour brainstorming answers to the questions that begin on the next page.

This project is a continuation of the book's first pen-and-paper brainstorming exercise on page 10. You'll find this project especially helpful if you have been doing the book's exercises in chronological order, but it will also be perfectly relevant and useful if you've randomly completed about half the book's projects.

Ahead you will find a set of questions. Think of these questions as prompts designed to get your thoughts flowing and your pen moving. Consider each question, one by one, and write whatever comes to mind—even if this means letting your responses drift into uncharted and unexpected territory. Spend between forty-five minutes and an hour filling your pages with whatever thoughts and ideas come to mind.

- Which, if any, of the exercises reminded you of artistic talents that been under-practiced and under-appreciated during the past few (or many) years?
- If you work professionally as an artist or a designer, which projects have brought to light techniques and tactics that could be applied to real-world jobs?
- Which projects resulted in pieces of art that you were most eager to put on the wall or share with others?

- Which of the book's projects were the most fun?
- What about expanding one of the book's projects and creating a set of pieces that could be put on display at home, in the office, in a cafe or in an art gallery? How could the project be modified to better fit your own interests, skills and ideals? (Consider making quick sketches as you brainstorm this material—sketches that will help you develop and remember the ideas that are coming to mind.)

- Have any of the projects left you feeling discouraged? If so, why? (Are we not just experimenting and trying out new things here? What's the big deal about "failing," anyway? Are you on board with the goal of not allowing feelings like this to creep into any of the upcoming projects?)
- Looking back at the book's activities you've completed so far, what are some ways media and techniques from some activities might be blended with media or techniques from other activities? What about trying out an idea or two before moving ahead with the rest of the book's projects?
- Which of your current set of creative skills do you especially hope to develop and sharpen in the months and years ahead?

Finish this activity the same way you did the book's first brainstorming exercise: by sealing your writings in an envelope. Store the envelope with the first one and forget about them, for now, anyway—you'll be reminded to fetch both when you get to the book's final brainstorming project on page 238.

The best creative projects often begin with a sketch made during a brief moment of inspiration.

MINI MOVIE. Don't have enough money or time to fund, shoot, edit and distribute that feature film you've always wanted to make? Fine. There is a byte-sized alternative: How about making a mini digital movie instead? All you'll need is a smartphone, a pocket digital camera, a camcorder or a DSLR that can shoot video along with video editing software (many computers come with this pre-installed, and several free and cheap video apps are available online). As far as distribution goes, well, that's easy these days: Ever hear of YouTube, Facebook or Vimeo?

Sample mini movies have been posted here:
WWW.JIMKRAUSEDESIGN.COM/D30

CAMERA

COMPUTER & VIDEO SOFTWARE

Activity 17: Mini movie. This project could be done with a simple smartphone video camera and basic editing software, or it could be done using a high-quality video camera and sophisticated software: It all depends on what you have access to and what you are comfortable using. The main thing is this: Use what you've got and make the most of it.

Video (as mentioned on pages 82–83) is an especially enticing and relevant media for artists of all kinds since it makes use of—and exercises—a broad range of creative skills. If you've never really made a video before (something more ambitious than, say, a straight-up recording of a kid's birthday party), this exercise will give you the chance to see for yourself how fun, rewarding and approachable this media can be. If you already have experience with videos and editing, use this project to flex your skills and also to affirm the idea that you *do* have the time to make full-length, broadcast quality movies—especially if you accept that a minute or two is an adequate length for a film and that websites like YouTube, Vimeo and Facebook are worthy venues for distributing your creations.

Of all the things needed to make a movie, the most important are these four: a good idea, a good eye, a digital camera that can shoot video and a computer with video editing software. Sure, things like video-capable DSLRs with various lenses, good sound recording equipment, a mobile lighting unit, a special effects department, actors and stylists are also nice things to have at one's disposal, but none are mandatory. So, for now, let's focus on the four must-haves—because really, these are all you need to get your butt off the couch and into the director's chair.

A good idea. What makes an idea a good movie idea? A movie idea can be good if it amounts to eye-pleasing imagery, brain-engaging content, funnybone-tickling humor, hair-raising frights or a combination of any of the above. What would you like your mini movie to be about? Your idea need not be complex (and it probably shouldn't be too complicated given the goal of keeping this thing down to a minute or two in length). What about a quick and instructive documentary on something simple like expertly sharpening a pencil or making a perfect chocolate chip cookie? How about a purely visual exposé on a favorite urban, suburban or natural setting? Could you arrange an interview with an especially interesting friend or co-worker? Think this over before you begin, and then: *begin*.

A good eye. It's extremely important to put everything you know about composition and aesthetics into every shot you record with a video camera. Don't be lazy with this one: Aesthetic excellence and visual originality are what set the great videos apart from the merely good ones.

A digital camera. Use whatever you own or can borrow. These days, most smartphone cameras—and nearly all pocket digital cameras—are capable of shooting high-definition video that looks surprisingly good when shown on computers and even on large-screen televisions. Keep in mind, however, that while the picture quality of these cameras may be quite good, the quality of the sound they record may or may not be so great: It all depends on what kinds

of sounds you'll be recording and under what conditions (high quality sound recordings generally require higher-quality recording equipment). One way to avoid sound issues is to make a movie that does not feature spoken dialogue or difficult-to-record sounds, and to then overlay the entire video with music and/or narration that's been recorded cleanly.

Video editing software. Video software makes it very easy to select, trim and arrange filmed clips into continuous streams of video. It also simplifies the process of improving the look of your footage, adding audio material, incorporating typographic elements and generating special effects.

There's a good chance that your computer or camera came with video editing software of some kind. If not, consider either buying software or downloading a free program (either way, do a thorough Web search to find out what the best products currently are). If you've never worked with video editing software, then embrace the opportunity this project will give you

 to learn more about an extremely relevant and increasingly accessible media.

Enough talk about movie-making for now: It's time to brainstorm, shoot and edit a mini movie of your own. Take a look at the thoughts and tips on the facing page, brainstorm for subject matter and then get started. A project like this could take several hours to complete, so make a point of keeping at it regularly until you are finished. You'll be glad you did, and who knows, this might be the start of a whole new creative outlet.

Don't be intimidated by the countless variables that surround the making of even a simple video: Just jump headlong into this exercise and see what happens. Here are a few thoughts to consider as you plan, shoot and edit your mini movie.

- Remember the lessons learned in Activity #9, Thinking in Edits, beginning on page 76? How about creating this activity's movie from a series of quick clips as well? Record your action from multiple points of view and edit your shots together afterwards.
- Consider making a quick storyboard of what you'll be shooting before you begin. Or, just wing it. Go with whatever method feels right to you.
- Shoot more than enough footage. That way you'll have plenty of clips to choose from when it comes time to edit and assemble the video.
- Get close to the action. A common shortcoming of amateur films is that the scenes all feature people and things that appear too small in the frame.
- Plan on devoting a surprising amount of time to the post-shooting phase of the project where you will be sitting at the computer selecting, editing and fine tuning your footage.
- Think about converting your video to black and white, boosting its color, heightening its contrast or applying a special filter or treatment.
- Take seriously the possibility of adding music to your video: music can be surprisingly capable of transforming the mundane into the magnificent.
- Use whatever design skills you possess to add good looking titles and end-credits to your mini movie.

Activity
#**18**
CATEGORY:
COMPOSITION

PLAYING WITH FIRE. This activity will train and reinforce a variety of highly employable skills involving the dexterity of your hands and the ability of your eyes to assess aesthetic characteristics such as flow, balance and grace. Also being trained here are skills that might put you in high demand during non-working hours: For one thing, you might find yourself without equal when it comes to crafting expressive fiery designs that could be airbrushed onto friends' Harleys, hot rods and Hula-Hoops.

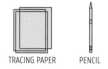
TRACING PAPER   PENCIL

Activity 18: Playing with fire. In this exercise, the focus is on the skills of the hand and the aesthetic sense of the eyes, and all you'll need to begin is a pencil and pad of tracing paper (a computer is optional, and even if you decide to use one, you won't need to turn it on until the bulk of the project has been completed).

① The flames we'll be drawing in this activity will be composed of three basic types of curves: S-shaped, C-shaped and U-shaped (both with and without flared tops). Fill the better part of a page with variations of these kinds of curves to get your hand accustomed to rendering them with grace and fluidity. ② Prepare for the work ahead by drawing an ellipse with a sharp pencil—an ellipse that is about 3" tall by however wide you choose to make it.

③ Set your elllpse under a fresh piece of tracing paper. Next, draw a U-shaped line that follows the outer edges of the ellipse except for where it flares outward at its upper ends. ④ Add a few S-shaped lines within the U-shaped enclosure (and feel free to include more than two curves in your S-shaped lines). Extend the curvy lines to the edges of the ellipse. The lines being drawn here will act as a framework for the flames being drawn in step 6 and beyond. ⑤ Add a few shorter S-shaped curves to fill out the ellipse's interior.

Think like a designer as you work. Think: variation, harmony, grace, balance, expression.

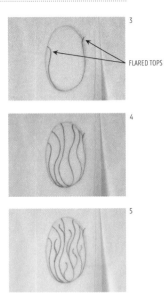

FLARED TOPS

145

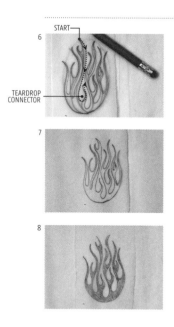

START

6

TEARDROP
CONNECTOR

7

8

⑥ Place a fresh piece of tracing paper over the skeletal framework you've just made. Begin drawing a flame: Start at its peak and draw gracefully downward using one of the underlying skeletal lines as a guide, and then, just before the pencil runs into another skeletal branch, make a graceful teardrop bowl that transitions the line to the next S-curve, continue the line upward to that flame's peak. Repeat this process throughout your design. Hint: It helps if you think of all your lines as modified S-shapes and all your connectors as teardrops. ⑦ A first draft, minus its underlying skeletal guidelines. ⑧ Improve your flames' appearance with at least one more tracing and then fill in its form. Done. Save this sketch for the optional digital follow-up on the next spread.

⑨ How about starting again, and this time creating a more complex design—one with small bits of flame springing from its upper regions?

⑩ What about using an asymmetrical teardrop to define the outer shape of your flame (as opposed to the ellipse that was used previously)?

⑪ Why not try using rectangular, square, circular or triangular outer dimensions?

What if you made a habit of doodling fiery designs like these? This is a great exercise for improving the dexterity of your hand as well as your eyes' ability to evaluate lines, shapes, balance and flow. Be sure to save drawings like this for potential reference and use in the future.

It's usually best to begin free-flowing drawings like these with pencil and paper before moving to the computer for finalization. Once this drawing had been scanned and brought into Illustrator, ellipses were added to the image to help determine the exact form of its inner curves. Cut-out portions of these ellipses were joined to lines drawn with Illustrator's PEN tool to create the flame's final form.

And remember, once a design has been created in Illustrator, that's really just the beginning: Explore all kinds of finalization options and consider a full range of outcomes. Each of the creations on the facing page was made from the computer-drawn outline of the flame shown at left.

149

Activity
19

CATEGORY:
INK AND PAINT

KID STUFF. Remember the colorful and artful creations you used to come up with as a kid using crayons, ink, colored paper and glue? Well, now's your chance to show your inner child who's boss by whipping out a few basic art supplies and using them in ways that take full advantage of everything you've learned since kindergarten about art, illustration, composition and life. And by the way, because of the inherent fun and nostalgia offered throughout this activity's exercises, these projects are especially well-suited to doing with a friend. How about hosting an "art date" with someone special?

WATERCOLOR PAPER · CRAYONS · BRUSH · INDIA INK · NAIL OR PIN · WATERCOLORS · STRAW (OPT.) · GOOGLY EYES (OPT.) · FINGER PAINT (OPT.)

Activity 19: Kid stuff. Ordinary typing paper will work for this project, but a thicker and toothier grade of drawing or watercolor paper would be best. Beyond that, all you'll need is a basic set of crayons, some India ink, a cheap thick brush (one that you don't mind using with ink) and a small picture-hanging nail or a pin.

① These instructions will be brief: You've probably done a project or two like this when you were in grade school. Start by using crayons to draw densely-colored designs on two or three small pieces of watercolor paper. Leave about a half inch of crayon-free area around each design, but other than that, no paper should be left showing.

② Next, paint a layer of India ink over your designs. Allow the ink to dry thoroughly. (A hair dryer may be used to speed the drying process.)

③ Grab a pin, a needle or a sharp nail (such as the small picture-hanging nail shown here). ④ Next you'll be drawing with your sharp-tipped tool by scratching through the layer of dried ink to reveal the colors beneath. The trick, of course, will be to scratch just hard enough to reach colors, but not so hard that you dig down to paper. What would you like to draw? An image? A pattern? An abstraction? It's totally up to you. Try something different for each piece. ⑤ Fun, isn't it?

Remember this illustration technique and keep supplies on hand: It might be the perfect solution for an upcoming personal or professional project.

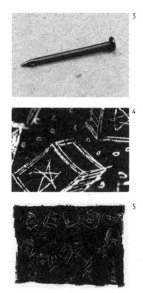

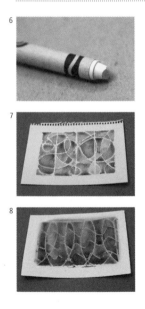

⑥ Here's another project that you can do with a crayon—a white crayon in particular. ⑦+⑧ The first step is difficult to show since it involves drawing on white paper with a white crayon, so instead of providing step-by-step visuals, here's a quick summary: Take your white crayon and draw—on watercolor paper—a free-flowing abstract design with plenty of areas of overlap. Next, apply watercolors to your design and watch as the paint refuses to adhere to the crayon's lines. The results can be surprisingly sophisticated and eye catching.

How about using colors that mimic what's in your living room? That way, your artwork is all the more likely to look at home when you hang it there.

Here are a couple more kid-stuff art projects to save for a rainy day when you and a fun-loving grown-up (or kid) are looking for something crafty to do. ⑨ This one is as silly as it is expressive and fun. Grab a sheet of butcher paper, put on a craft apron, add some small puddles of ink to the paper and use a straw to blow the ink into a bunch of crazy configurations. Add plastic googly eyes (easily found at craft stores) to some of the ink splats and then cut out the designs to create a herd of mythical beasts for the front of your refrigerator. (See Activity 23, Masterpieces Galore, page 178 for more ink blowing ideas.) ⑩ Finger painting, anyone? All you need is a large piece of paper, some fingers and some finger paints.

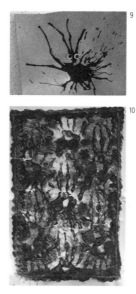

9

10

So what if the art techniques highlighted in this activity are used by school children the world over? These methods of visual expression are valid and effective styles of illustration that can be (and are) regularly employed by designers to create communicative images, attractive backdrop artwork and decorative patterns for professional projects. How about keeping a drawer at your office stocked with basic art supplies: **paints, inks and papers that could be used to create pieces of art that perfectly meet the needs of real-world jobs?** And, just because these supplies will **supposedly** be dedicated to purely professional purposes, that doesn't mean they can't be pulled out of their drawers during office parties and for after-hours craft projects, **right?**

Activity

20

CATEGORY:
HAND AND EYE

POSITIVELY NEGATIVE. Ever look at something like a chair or a bicycle and—instead of trying to focus on the object itself—train your attention on the empty spaces within and around the object? As Betty Edwards writes in her famous book, *Drawing on the Right Side of the Brain*, artists who give attention to these negative spaces when rendering a subject grant priority to parts of the brain that see actual shapes—as opposed to giving precedence to the know-it-all parts of the mind that tend to influence the hand with pre-ordained ideas of how a subject is "supposed" to look. This exercise will give you an excellent chance to experience these negative spaces in a positive way.

BICYCLE   SKETCH PAD   PENCIL

Activity 20: Positively negative. A bicycle would be great subject matter for this activity, as would any other object that has plenty of negative spaces (interior openings within the object's form): a chair, a stool or an eggbeater, for instance. Place a sketch pad in your lap or on a tabletop and use a pencil when drawing for this exercise.

①+② Before beginning to draw in earnest, sit down in front of your subject and look for negative spaces within and around its form (some of these shapes have been highlighted at lower left). It may take several minutes to shut down the parts of your brain that insist on focusing on your subject's physical form, so create a few sketches of its negative spaces to help activate the more intuitive and non-literal centers of your mind (and be patient with yourself if this process takes time).

③ When you feel ready, begin drawing your entire subject—by *only* drawing the negative spaces within and around it. ④ Above all, don't worry if your drawing does not look quite right (or even if it looks completely wrong). The goal here is simply to engage and exercise connections between your eyes and hand in order to enhance your ability to more accurately see and render objects from life.

Waiting for a dentist appointment? Riding a bus? How about using downtime like this to look for— and possibly sketch—some of the negative spaces in your surroundings? Your ability to see and render the shapes that exist between, within and around objects will improve with practice.

EXTERIOR SHAPES, INTERIOR SPACES

Not only is it beneficial to pay attention to negative spaces when drawing or sketching dimensional subjects, it's also important to take both interior and exterior shapes into account when working with two-dimensional creations. Skilled typographers are especially mindful of interactions between negative and positive shapes. Take a look at the differences between the interior and exterior forms of these numerical characters from the font families of Caslon, Goudy, Hoefler and Times Roman. The differences—and associations— between these numerals' negative and positive shapes amount to the distinctions that set each character apart from the others.

Activity
21

PERSONAL MONOGRAM. Monograms play a dual visual role. For one thing, they act as typographic placeholders for the name of a person, organization or business. They also serve as carriers of thematic conveyances, as in the case of this playfully macabre capital A built from bones. What about creating a monogram for yourself, and how about designing it in a way that conveys aspects of who you are or things you like to do? This activity may take a few hours to complete. Begin now with a brainstorming session and some sketches, and finish later on using software, hands-on media or a combination of both.

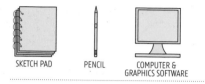

SKETCH PAD   PENCIL   COMPUTER & GRAPHICS SOFTWARE

Activity 21: Personal monogram. Use a sketch pad and a pen to begin the brainstorming and thumbnail portions of this project. Later, you'll most likely be finishing your monogram using a program like Illustrator or Photoshop, but traditional tools such as brushes, paper, watercolors or ink should also be considered.

① The monogram you create for this exercise can feature one or more of your initials. Keep this in mind as you begin brainstorming ideas.

Author's note: The samples featured on this spread and the two that follow have been borrowed from my previous book, The Logo Brainstorm Book. *These samples have been included to help launch ideas in your head as you ponder options for your own design.*

166   Activity 21

TIME NEEDED:
A COUPLE HOURS OR MORE

② Begin brainstorming ways of designing your personal monogram by making lists of things that build a picture of who you are: favorite activities, interests, beliefs, art, music, books, places, food, styles, and more. Next, look over your lists and see what appeals most. Maybe it's one thing in particular, maybe it's more than one thing and maybe it's a visual or conceptual melding of ideas. Record anything that comes to mind in the form of quick thumbnail sketches. The sketches do not need to be neat or detailed—these are just shorthand idea-savers for later on. Remember: There are all kinds of ways of presenting monograms—cover many options with your sketches.

2

④ After you have a few promising thumbnails to consider, begin narrowing things down until you get to the one idea that feels most worthy of finalization. ⑤ Once on the computer, be sure to explore font options for your monogram. Create whatever typographic, symbol-based or decorative elements are required to complete your design using exactly the skills you possess and whatever tools you need (digital, photographic or otherwise).

Use the samples on the next three pages to help generate your own monogram ideas.

Activity

22

CATEGORY:
COLOR

WARM AND COOL. Colors have temperatures. Blue
and violet are cool tones that tend to deliver calming
conveyances of rest and quietude. Red, yellow and orange
are warm hues that ably transmit notions of action and
vigor. Grays can be tinted with warming and cooling
hues, and artists who can clearly see and evaluate the
differences between warm and cool grays are not only
able to construct appealing palettes from these hues,
they are also able to use them as effective backdrops for
intense colors. Use this exercise to boost your ability to
assess and appreciate grays of a variety of temperatures
and temperaments.

WATERCOLOR PAD   PENCIL   BRUSH   WATERCOLORS   PAINT MIXING TRAY   WATER JAR   RAG OR PAPER TOWEL

Activity 22: Warm and cool. Watercolors would be the best choice for this exercise, but acrylics that have been thinned with water or acrylic medium would work just fine, too. Also needed: a small piece or pad of watercolor paper, a pencil, a fine brush, a watercolor tray (something like an old mini-muffin tin can also be used as a paint tray) a jar of water and a rag.

① Use a pencil to draw a grid on your piece of watercolor paper. Leave white space between your grid and the edge of the paper. The grid shown here is eight rectangles across and six rectangles down. Yours could be the same, similar or completely different. ② Create a small pool of watery black paint. Aim for a mixture that dries as a medium-value gray.

③ Fill every-other rectangle of your grid with a wash of black paint. Allow variations in the value of the black by adding more paint to some rectangles and less to others. Work as quickly as you can without sacrificing quality—the idea here is to keep the paint at least slightly wet as you move on to the next pair of steps. ④+⑤ Paint the remaining rectangles in the same way with more watery black paint. For the most part, leave a very thin white gap between the rectangles, but occasionally allow your brush to connect a pair of rectangles so that wet paint can spread between them. This will give your design a nice watercolor look. Allow the paint to dry (use a blow dryer or a lightbulb to speed the drying process, if you like).

3

4

5

At this stage, your artwork should look something like this. Now it's time to add some visual energy and interest to the design by tinting its various rectangles with a contrasting assortment warm and cool tints. Do this by applying watery, transparent washes of color to each rectangle. Lend a warm cast to some of the spaces with hues that tend toward red, yellow, orange, burgundy or brown. Cool the appearance of other rectangles by applying light washes that lean toward blue, violet or blue-green. Add your tints to the design in whatever order and arrangement you like best. Subtlety is the goal here: Keep your color washes light and transparent (if a certain rectangle's tint ends up being *too* subtle, give it another wash of color).

Cool grays
are those that
contain hints
of blue, violet
or blue-green.

Neutral gray
(sometimes called
achromatic gray)
has no color cast
whatsoever.

Warm grays
convey hints
of yellow,
red, orange
or brown.

A few miscellaneous thoughts about gray.

Grays have temperatures that range from cool to neutral to warm. The temperature of a gray is generally relative: For example, a slightly warm gray may appear cool when paired with a very warm gray. *Gray* need not equal *boring:* It's all a matter of a how a gray is—or a set of grays are—used. A palette of subtle and intriguing intensity can be created by combining grays of various visual temperatures. A warm accent color (such as a vibrant orange) can appear all the more lively when it is supported by a contrasting backdrop of cool grays. Conversely, the calming conveyances of a light and bright cool hue can be emphasized by placing it against a visually simmering backdrop of dark, warm grays. Some artists refer to certain tans, beiges and browns as warm grays—it's a distinction that generally lies in the eye of the beholder.

MASTERPIECES GALORE. Most people who regularly use a camera are well-versed at cropping unsightly or unneeded areas from photographs. In this exercise, cropping will be employed for similar reasons, only here the process will be applied in a greatly exaggerated way, as numerous tiny compositional croppings are selected from within a giant piece of abstract art. While working on this project, keep in mind that even though ink and paper are the media of choice for this project, the same method of finding eye-catching croppings from within large-scale creations could be applied in all kinds of ways using other media.

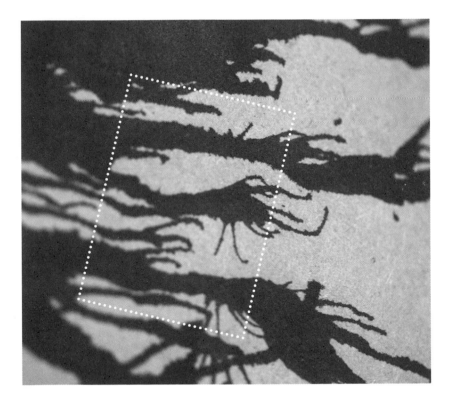

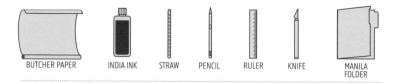

BUTCHER PAPER INDIA INK STRAW PENCIL RULER KNIFE MANILA FOLDER

Activity 23: Masterpieces galore. This project can get a bit messy, and India ink can be tough to clean up, so protect your work table with cardboard or with a couple layers of newsprint or butcher paper. Also, a craft apron would be an excellent thing to wear over the top of the less-than-precious clothing you wear while working.

① Spread a large sheet of butcher paper across the top of your well-protected work surface and put a small puddle of ink somewhere on the sheet.

② Next, pick up a straw (the thinner the better: coffee stirring straws are ideal), take in a big breath and direct a blast of air through the straw and at the puddle of ink. Blow hard and chase the little tendrils of ink across the paper to create wild, uncontrolled and artful explosions of ink.

③ Fill your large sheet of paper with branching, twisting, merging and diverging trajectories of ink. Let the ink dry. ④ Do you still have the cardboard mask created for activity #6? If so, get it. If not, make one (directions are on page 52). Move your mask across the surface of your spattered sheet of paper and locate small and attractive abstract compositions. Seek a variety of looks for the abstractions (busy, plain, dark, light, etc.) and use a pen to outline favorite croppings as you go. Find and outline at least a couple dozen of these mini-masterpieces. ⑤ When you're done searching and selecting, use a ruler and an art knife to cut out individual croppings (protect your table from cuts with a sturdy piece of cardboard while cutting).

MANILA FOLDER MASK

When all is finished, you'll have two things: a large ink-spattered sheet of butcher paper minus a bunch of rectangular holes and a collection of tiny ink-on-paper works of art. How about putting your assortment of playing-card-size abstractions on display using string, thumbtacks and paper clips?

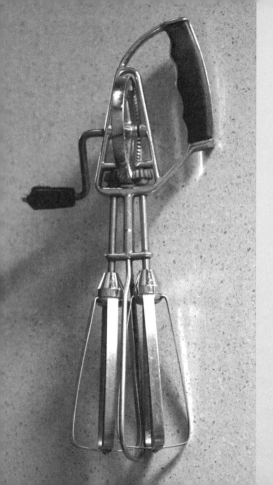

What about re-inventing this exercise using a slightly different set of rules and wholly different media? Here's how: Select a nearby object. Any object. Big or small, beautiful or plain, complex or simple. Next, take your camera and look for at least a couple dozen interesting views of the subject. The views could be from near, from far, or, maybe best of all, from a mix of both near and far. Use your designer's eye for composition and your intuitive sense for eye-catching beauty to record your photos. This is a truly great exercise to try anytime you have some time—and a camera—on hand: It'll sharpen your design sense and your photography skills while producing an intriguing set of related images.

Activity

24

CATEGORY:
HAND AND EYE

LETTING GO, REIGNING IN. As designers, most of us like to maintain as much control as we can when managing clients' unforgiving deadlines, absolute goals and expectations of perfection. It should come as a relief, then, to learn that this exercise is all about letting go. Sound like fun? It will be. Sound a little intimidating or uncomfortable? Don't worry about it: Even though the artwork you'll be creating will begin with a flurry of wild-and-free brush strokes, it will end by providing ways of reigning in your unbridled creative output to produce an illustration that's akin to a tame lion: equal parts wild animal and domesticated pussy cat.

PAPER: SEVERAL SHEETS | BRUSH | INDIA INK | SCISSORS | TAPE | CAMERA OR SCANNER | COMPUTER & PHOTOSHOP

Activity 24: Letting go, reigning in. Gather the supplies shown above. This project's samples were created with the well-used watercolor brush shown

at left. Use a similar fine or medium tipped art brush. Be sure to protect your work surface from stains with butcher paper or newsprint.

① Take a look at the saxophone pictured on pages 192–193. Ponder its form for a minute or two and absorb the essential gestures of just what it is that makes a saxophone a saxophone. Next, with a sheet of paper in front of you, dip your brush in ink and render a free-flowing abstraction of the instrument using quick and confident strokes. Don't try to copy the instrument precisely: The idea here is to capture the essence and the spirit of a sax using brush and ink. Set the paper aside to dry.

② Repeat the previous step at least a couple dozen times. Try out different styles; fill each sheet with an entire instrument or with repetitions of a certain detail. Shut down the critical parts of your brain as you work and let the ink flow freely and intuitively. Chances are, you will like parts of certain renderings without falling in love with any of them as a whole. Don't panic: There's a solution.

③ Once all the ink has dried, take a thoughtful look at everything you have produced and identify favorite details and sections from your renderings. Use a pair of scissors to cut out these favored parts and set the clippings aside.

④ Your goal is to come up with a collection of pieces that can be assembled into a single good-looking whole.

⑤+⑥ Use bits of transparent tape to assemble a complete illustration on a fresh sheet of paper (avoid letting the tape overlap any ink since this might cause problems later on when the assemblage is photographed or scanned). Don't worry if the various pieces of your rendering don't connect perfectly or if there are small gaps between them: These imperfections will be handled digitally once the composite illustration is imported into Photoshop. ⑦ When you are satisfied with the look of your creation, photograph or scan the artwork and import it into Photoshop (Elements could also be used).

⑧ Use Photoshop's **LEVELS** or **CURVES** controls to give your artwork a pure white backdrop and to adjust the darkness and consistency of its inked lines. (**THRESHOLD** controls could also be used to convert the rendering to a purely black and white image). Use the **ERASER** and **PENCIL** tools to remove unwanted artifacts from the image and to repair awkward connections between joined segments of your creation. ⑨ How about creating, scanning and importing an expressive spattering of ink as a finishing touch? Are there digital treatments that could be applied as final enhancements? What about adding a photographic, colored, textural or typographic backdrop to your illustration?

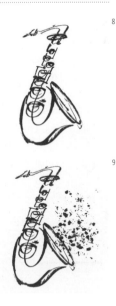

8

9

BRUSHES

If you are new to painting and have enjoyed working with brushes for this book's exercises, then you may be starting to sense the power and versatility these real-world tools can bring to your design work—especially when they are combined with the digital tools and the know-how you already possess. How about taking the time to become better acquainted with the many different types of brushes (as well as non-traditional paint-delivery devices like cotton swabs and toothbrushes)? Start your own collection with low-cost brushes and paintbrush alternatives and populate it over time with tools that best fit your preferences.

GOING IN CIRCLES. This project will exercise
your camera skills, while also providing a good workout
for your aptitudes of observation and resourcefulness.
And, as if that were not reason enough to get excited
about the project ahead, know also that it's an activity
that can be done with virtually no preparation. Once
completed, this project will leave you in possession
of an exceptionally eye-catching collection of display-
ready images *and* the raw material needed to make a
captivating stop-motion video such as the sample posted
here: WWW.JIMKRAUSEDESIGN.COM/D30. Interested? Of course
you are. Grab your best camera and read on.

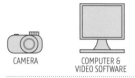

CAMERA   COMPUTER & VIDEO SOFTWARE

Activity 25: Going in circles. Use the best camera you have—whether that's a smartphone camera, a pocket digital camera or a DSLR. Photo editing software such as Photoshop or Elements may be used to finalize your images. Basic video-editing or slideshow software will be needed to assemble everything into a stop-motion video made from your images.

This is going to be fun and simple: Use your camera to take a picture of anything you can find nearby that is round or spherical. Your individual subjects may be large or small, plain or complex and they may be sought indoors or out. Open drawers and closets to find photo-worthy material. Look on shelves and inside drawers. Look at signage, vehicles and fabrics. Work methodically and carefully: Subject matter should be there in abundance if you take the time to find it.

Consider shooting each of your subjects in a way that fills the viewfinder with a similarly sized— and similarly centered—circle. This may mean using your camera's close-up setting so that you can help tiny objects take up more space in the frame, and it may also mean stepping back from larger things. And whatever you do, don't just line up the camera and pull the trigger when you see a good subject: Make an effort to record each image as a stand-alone, attractive photograph worthy of display. Keep at this until you have between thirty and a hundred images.

The images shown on these spreads were shot using a DSLR with a 50mm lens.

Finished taking pictures? Import your photos into a program like Photoshop or Elements. Adjust each photo's contrast and color as needed to give the set a consistent look—whether you decide to go with color, black-and-white or tinted images. Want your images to appear identical in size and position when they're assembled into a video? Now is the time to crop them as needed to accomplish this goal. (The images shown on this spread have been cropped in this way.)

The pictures you've shot will now be assembled into a stop-motion movie (a video made from a sequence of photos that are each on-screen for anywhere from a quarter-second to several seconds).

Most video editing and slide show software will allow you to assemble still photographs into fast-moving sequences of images. Not sure what program to use? Do a search for "free stop-motion software" and you will find several options. Common video editing programs like iMovie, Final Cut Pro and Premiere also offer stop-motion options. Presentation software such as PowerPoint and Keynote can generate stop-motion videos as well.

As you finalize your stop-motion video, play around with the timing of your images and also with the addition of titles and music. How about posting your finished project online?

CREATIVE CAPTIONING. It's interesting to see what happens when words are added to images. This is especially true when the words bring up unexpected thoughts or ideas, rather than merely providing the viewer with an obvious caption for what they can already see. The challenge here is exactly that—to add words to images borrowed from your personal photo cache in order to create visuals that are capable of delivering conveyances and messages that go beyond what either the words or the photographs could have delivered on their own.

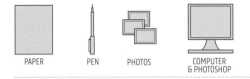

PAPER   PEN   PHOTOS   COMPUTER & PHOTOSHOP

Activity 26: Creative captioning. A dictionary and a thesaurus (electronic or paper) may help get the ideas flowing for this exercise. The photos used could come from your cache of existing images or they could be shot specifically for this project—it's up to you. Software such as Photoshop or Elements will be need to finalize your images and to add type.

① If you own a digital camera, then, chances are, you also have a large (and growing) collection of images on one or more hard drives. Go to your collection(s) and look for photos that especially appeal to you—either visually, conceptually, emotionally or all of the above. Look for about a dozen photos that you are particularly fond of and copy them into a folder of their own.

② Now brainstorm. Begin by opening your images and arranging them on a screen or by printing a copy of each. Get a notepad or a piece of paper and start writing down whatever comes to mind when you look at your photos, one by one. What single-word descriptors come to mind? What statements? What thoughts? What themes? What sensible labels? What nonsensical quips or inside jokes? How about looking for suitable quotations online? Write down good ideas, bad ideas and half-formed ideas—anything that pops into your head. Your goal here is to come up with especially intriguing textual material that could be added to about half of your photographs.

③ Next, distill and perfect. Choose the most promising words and ideas from your lists. Refine what you have by asking yourself, *Is there a more impactful, interesting, funny or serious way of saying what I'm trying to say through this image and these words?* Look to a thesaurus for alternatives to some of your words: Maybe you'll locate an offshoot that's better than what you originally had in mind. Aim for solutions that are unique, interesting and insightful, and work hard to avoid those that are cheesy or overly obvious. Keep at this until you feel like you have at least one strong textual candidate for between four and eight of your images.

④+⑤ Finally, use image-editing software to combine your words and images in attractive ways. Use your computer and software to thoroughly explore the options. Typeface or hand-lettered? Large type or small? Opaque or translucent letters? White or colored? Centered or non-centered? And what about the photo itself? Color, black-and-white or tinted? A special effect?

A few more examples of text-plus-image samples are featured on the next spread. Use those, and the ones that have already been shown in this section, to help generate ideas as you work.

i think
i can

This project is
a very practical
exercise for anyone
involved in graphic
design. Clever pairings
between images and
titles, captions or
quotes can be used
for projects like CD
packages, book covers,
magazine articles,
advertisements
and posters.

Tired.

Let nothing be lost upon you. Be always searching for new sensations. Be afraid of nothing.

OSCAR WILDE

....

INSTANT PHOTO STUDIO. Although some photography websites and magazines might have you believe otherwise, more is not always better. In fact, not only is it possible to shoot attractive studio photographs without high-powered lights, remotely-fired flash units, the latest DSLR and a pricey lens, it's actually *very* doable. In fact, artful still-life photos can be captured using only a piece of matboard as a backdrop, a nearby window for light and a pocket digital camera to shoot with. Hard to believe? It's true: The only piece of "specialty" equipment used to capture the shot at right was a tripod—and even that was optional.

CAMERA | TRIPOD | CHAIR | MATBOARD OR FABRIC | TIME NEEDED: ABOUT AN HOUR AND A HALF

Activity 27: Instant photo studio. This chapter's photos were shot using the setup shown at right. Your own setup may differ, but the important points are these: use a window for light; use a piece of matboard or a sheet of fabric as a backdrop; use a digital camera (pocket, DSLR or something in between) and steady the camera with a tripod or by setting it on a solid surface.

Begin by putting together an in-home or an in-office photo studio in the manner of the setup shown at right. If you don't have a large sheet of black matboard to use as a backdrop, drape a dark piece of fabric over something large and flat. ① Next, how about heading outdoors with a pair of scissors to collect some photogenic organic subject matter? (Or, if it's easier, run down to a florist's shop or grocery store and collect your subject matter there.)

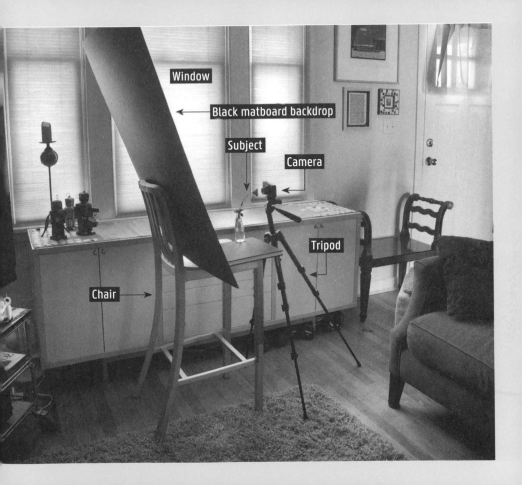

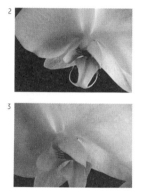

② Place your subject in a vase or clip it to something stable. Attach your camera to a tripod, put it in close-up mode and set the camera to shoot with a two-second delay (this will help ensure sharp images since pressing the shutter button might shake the camera slightly). Next, take pictures: Move both the camera and your subject as needed to obtain the most interesting and attractive shots of your subject.

③ If you know how to use your camera's controls, put it in aperture-priority mode so you can control the depth of field of your shots. Also, set the camera's ISO at 100 or 200 so that the photos will be free of graininess (this ISO setting might result in lengthy exposures—something you won't have to worry about since the camera is being steadied by a tripod).

④ If you are unfamiliar with your camera's controls (and if the previous paragraph made little or no sense to you) then consult your camera's manual and use this exercise as an opportunity to learn about—and to practice—aperture and ISO settings and exposure controls. ⑤ If you are using a pocket digital camera and would like to blur parts of your image with a shallow depth of field, try taking the camera out of close-up mode, pulling back from your subject, zooming in and using a low aperture setting. If you are shooting with a DSLR and have a 50mm or a 100mm lens, either of these will grant you extremely fine depth-of-field control.

4

5

⑥ A lighting tip: If you would like to add a touch of illumination to portions of your subject that are not facing the window, use a white sheet of paper to reflect light into that area. Give it a try—you'll probably be surprised how much light can be bounced onto a subject in this way. ⑦ How about experimenting with your camera's flash? (And why not? There's no penalty for "wasting" shots when shooting digitally.) Here's a neat trick: Use your finger or a piece of paper to cover parts of your camera's flash unit when shooting. A finger was used to cover the lower half of a pocket camera's flash when capturing the shot at left—thus creating a gradual transition to darkness in the photo's lower region.

⑧ Who says you have to photograph flowers from the front? What about aiming for a different perspective by turning your subject away from the lens? What other non-traditional points of view are worth considering? Keep your mind open to ideas as you work. ⑨ A bouquet of dead flowers: Again, why be ordinary? Dried and decaying plants offer beauty of a different sort through an abundance of interesting visual textures and intriguing forms.

*Record your photographs in color, and then, if you want to convert them to monochrome, import the images into Photoshop where you can take advantage of this program's powerful and versatile **BLACK & WHITE** controls.*

Like taking pictures? Keep a camera with you at all times: It's the best way to build a collection of images for both personal and professional use. Keep your eyes open for photo opportunities that involve interesting sights, attractive textures, intriguing compositions and communicative conveyances.

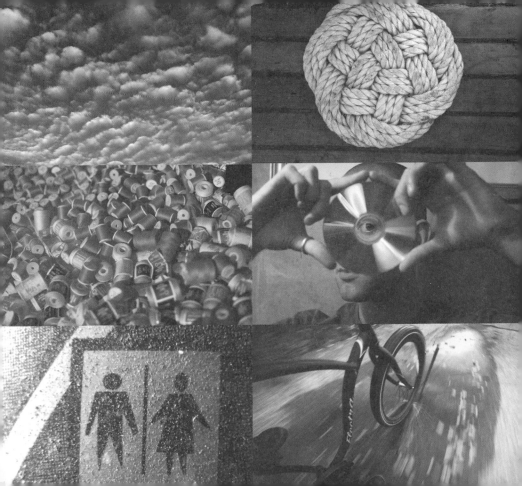

BALLOON BOWLS. When was the last time you made something with paper mache? Last Halloween? Last year? Last century? Now's your chance to be reminded of the good gooey fun that happens when flour, water and strips of newsprint are combined to create works of art. And we're not talking goofy chicken masks or crazy party piñatas here: We're talking display-ready bowls that will look right at home shelved next to the gallery-quality ceramics you bought at last summer's art fair. Prepare for this fun and crafty exercise by donning an art apron and covering your worktable with newsprint or butcher paper.

NEWSPAPER | WHITE FLOUR | PLASTIC CUP AND PLASTIC BOWL | BALLOONS | PAINT | BRUSH

Activity 28: Balloon bowls. Not much is needed to make paper mache: just water, white flour and newsprint (higher grade papers can also be used, as mentioned on page 227). A plastic bowl will also be needed, as will a package of party balloons, some acrylic paint and a brush. And don't forget to protect your work surface with butcher paper or newsprint.

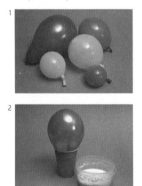

① Inflate several balloons to different sizes to prepare them for use as bowl-forming molds.

② Set a balloon in a plastic cup that's been weighted with a handful of pennies—this will help keep the cup steady as you work with the balloon. You won't need the paper mache paste until step 5, but go ahead and prepare the mixture now: In a plastic bowl, mix two cups of water with one cup of white flour and a dash of salt (salt prevents mold from forming later on) and stir or whisk thoroughly.

③ Next, to further prepare for the upcoming steps, tear a few sheets of newsprint into strips that are roughly ¾" by 4" (no need to be exact here). ④ Apply a layer of these newsprint strips to your balloon: strips that have **been wetted only with water—no paste.** (There is the possibility of the balloon becoming a permanent part of your bowl if paste is used for the first layer of paper.) Apply your water-wetted strips of paper to the upper half of the balloon.

A few strips of newsprint plus flour and water: That's all it takes to make something with paper mache. Keep this in mind the next time you are looking to fill some downtime with an art project.

223

⑤ Ready to get your fingers gooey? Give your paste mixture a stir and dip a strip of paper into the bowl. Submerge the strip briefly and then lift it out with one hand while using fingers of your other hand to squeegee excess paste from the paper. Next, lay the strip onto the balloon and lightly smooth it into place. ⑥ Repeat this procedure until there are three or four layers of overlapping strips pasted to the upper half of the balloon. ⑦ Complete at least three bowls of different sizes in this way and let them dry for twenty-four hours.

Don't worry about making a nice edge to what will be your bowls' rims: A rough edge will lend a nice handcrafted look to your creations.

Last of all, paint your bowls in whatever creative
and artistic way you like. Acrylics would work well
since they can be covered with a protective coat of
either matte or gloss medium. Display the finished
bowls individually or as a stacked set. (Coins have
been added to the bottom bowl in this set to allow
it to support the others in an intriguing way.)

Interested in aiming for a more upscale outcome for a paper mache project? Consider some options in terms of the supplies you use and the techniques you apply. **This paper mache bowl was made from three different layers of handmade and custom-made papers.** Paper bowls could also be fabricated from discarded bits of gift wrap, ticket stubs, significant magazine articles, love letters or traffic tickets, just to name a few ideas.

DESKTOP MAKEOVER. The computer has become *the* tool of the trade for creative professionals of all kinds—designers included. And, since so many of us spend so much of our time looking at our computer screens, why not make an effort to personalize and enhance the look of things? All you'll need for this exercise is a computer, software (such as Illustrator, Photoshop or InDesign), some fonts and willingness to explore, experiment, craft and create.

COMPUTER
& SOFTWARE

Activity 29: Desktop makeover. A basic level of familiarity with Adobe Illustrator will be needed for this activity. If you are more familiar with Photoshop or InDesign, you could use either of these programs instead—just translate the following instructions (when necessary) to fit the way those programs work.

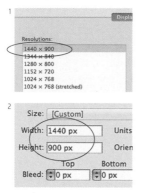

① The goal here will be to create some desktop images for your computer—images that could also be used as part of your screen-saver slide show. Begin by looking up your screen's resolution (search online or ask a computer-savvy friend if you need help finding this information).

② Next, open a new Illustrator document that matches the size of your screen.

TIME NEEDED:
ABOUT AN HOUR

③ Let's start by cleaning up Illustrator's list of
colors. Open the **SWATCHES** panel (*Window > Swatches*)
and choose *Select All Unused* from the panel's
upper-right pull-down menu (circled). Next, use
the same menu to select *Delete Swatch*. The panel's
list of colors should now be greatly simplified.
④ Go to the same pull-down menu as before
and select *New Swatch*. This will open the **SWATCH
OPTIONS** panel. Use this panel's sliders to formulate
an appealing hue. This color will be used as a
foundational hue for the image you're about to
create. (CMYK sliders have been used here since
many designers find it easier to adjust colors on-
the-fly with these sliders than with RGB sliders—
use whichever you prefer).

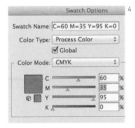

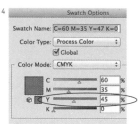

④ Colors that have slight but noticeable differences between them tend to look good as a set. Let's create five more colors that are each closely related to the hue you just created. Highlight your color in the **SWATCHES** panel, then select *Duplicate Swatch* from the **PANELS** pull-down menu. Double-click on the duplicate color to open the **SWATCH OPTIONS** panel and then move one of the sliders anywhere from ten to fifty percent. This should produce a new color that's a close relative of the first. Come up with a total of six closely-related hues in this way, and fine-tune each until you are happy with the set. Next, choose one more color: an accent hue that is decidedly different from the others.

⑤ With your palette of seven hues ready, turn your attention to Illustrator's font menu. Select asterisks from six notably different font families. Convert each asterisk to outlines (*Type > Create Outlines*). ⑥ Next, place each asterisk on a layer of its own and color each with a different hue from your custom-made palette. Also, create a rectangle that fills the document's backdrop, and color this rectangle with the remaining hue. All the components needed to build an eye-catching screen saver are now in place.

This exercise will produce one or two typographically-themed images. What about creating a few more and using the set as a screen-saver slide show?

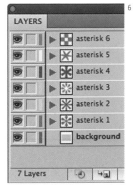

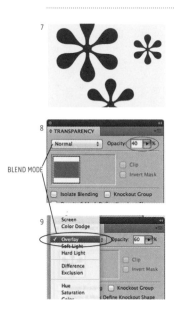

7

8

BLEND MODE

9

7 Turn off all but one of your asterisk-holding layers (leave the background layer visible and locked). Copy, resize and reposition the asterisk on the unlocked visible layer. Aim for an attractive mix of sizes and placements for this layer's contents. 8 + 9 Next, spend time adjusting the transparency and blend mode of each of the layer's asterisks. After that, turn on the other layers—one at a time—and apply the same treatments to the asterisks on those layers.

Hint: Lock all but the layer you are currently working with to make it easiest to select and alter items on that layer. Make adjustments to your overall composition until you love what you see.

(10) This is a great exercise for people who are fluent with Illustrator's controls since it provides these users with a chance to flex their creative talents while having fun with this program's deep set of features. If you are new to Illustrator's transparency effects and blend modes, then really dig into this project and explore your options: It won't take long to develop a good sense for how to best use these intuitive and powerful controls.

10

11

(11) How about applying more effects and treatments to your design? BLUR and GRADIENT effects have been used here to add notes of sophistication and depth.

What if *all* the background images and screen-savers on your computer were from personal art projects? The artwork could be of the digital variety, or it could be scanned images of things you've created using pens, paint or even pasta (see page 60). One especially nice thing about featuring art of

this kind on your computer is that it'll regularly offer pleasant reminders of your aptitude for creative expression outside the venue of for-profit creativity. Not only that, but coworkers and bosses may see these on-screen creations and think, *Hey, we could use talents like these for the work we do here...*

CONVERSATION WITH SELF, PART III.

So, what's next? You don't really want things to end here, now that you've come to the end of this book's projects, do you? Wouldn't you like to take the things you've learned—along with your newly invigorated determination to begin and complete personal art projects—and continue to make leaps toward dreamed-of creative objectives? Who wouldn't? Here's something you can do right here and right now to help prompt those leaps: Brainstorm using pen and paper to come up with ideas and plans that will help turn those possibilities into realities.

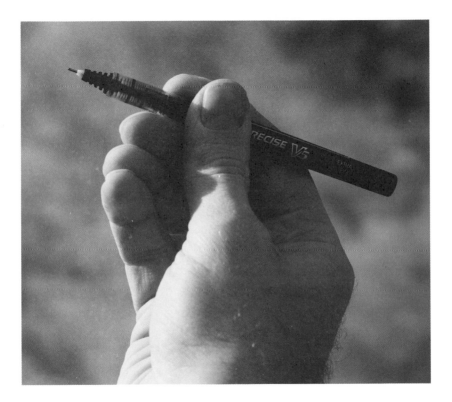

NOTEBOOK   PEN

....

Activity 30: Conversation with self, part III. This is the final exercise for
D30, so find a quiet spot to work and block out at least an hour of your
time. All you'll need is a pen, paper, a mind that's open to possibilities
and those two sealed envelopes that contain your thoughts from the
book's two previous brainstorm sessions (pages 10 and 128).

This will be a great way to wrap up the
exercises in *D30*—by brainstorming the future.
Hopefully you've already completed the two
previous brainstorming sessions before embarking
on this one, and also, ideally, you should have
already completed most or all of the book's exercises.

Begin by opening the envelopes that contain your earlier brainstormed
material and reading through it. A nice little time capsule, eh? A snapshot of
where you were in terms of your creative skills and aspirations before you
reached this point in the book and this day of your life.

When you looked through your previously written material, you may have been pleasantly reminded of goals and ideals that are still foremost in your mind. On the other hand, your goals and ideals may have shifted, expanded or changed. Whatever the case, here you are, and in a minute you'll have the chance to brainstorm and write about your up-to-date perspective on these matters—the specifics of which may evolve even as you write.

Go ahead and contemplate the content of your unsealed papers for a few minutes and then prepare to move ahead with one last brainstorming session.

Ready to write? First off, put pen to paper and write down some thoughts about your latest list of high-priority creativity-oriented goals and objectives. As mentioned earlier, this material may be similar to what you wrote before, and it may be different. Either way is fine: Go with the flow.

Next, brainstorm the specifics of projects you would absolutely love to begin—and finish—either in the very near or the distant future. Write about these projects and include details such as the skills you will need in order to complete the projects. Spend as much time as you need writing about these things before moving on.

Now write about actual detailed steps you'd like to follow to reach your highest priority objectives. Be specific. For instance, if you've decided you want to do more illustration work as part of your freelance gig as

a designer, and that you'll need to improve your painting skills to achieve this goal, then perhaps you'll need to create a to-do list that includes doing personal projects like portraits and still-life paintings; possibly taking classes or hiring a private instructor; seeking the critique of skilled artists; looking for opportunities to show your work publicly and gaining exposure once your skill level reaches a certain level of excellence.

In addition to filling in the details about your big-picture plans, write down any specific hardware, software or tools you'll need in order to get going. Don't let a lack of paint brushes, for example, keep you from painting and do what you can to get hold of good quality computers, cameras and software if your goals involve digital media. Also, make an effort to provide yourself with a good workspace if your home or office is lacking in this regard.

If your skills are already reasonably in line with what you want to achieve through them, then spend this time brainstorming ways in which your talents could be put to use in the here and now: Think about art you could create, messages you could convey, collections you could build, people you could show your work to and both digital and real-life venues through which your projects could be displayed.

Let this brainstorming session go wherever it takes you. Ideally, this session will leave you feeling excited, encouraged and more hopeful than ever about how your creative talents can be melded with your other meaningful life interests.

A parting message.

Making art a habit is a good thing. And since art happens most often when ready-to-use supplies are kept within easy reach, how about creating a dedicated art space? If you have the corner of a room to spare, for instance, then all you may need to do is pick up a work table from an art store or a second-hand store and put a few painting, drawing and craft supplies on nearby shelves. If you are tight on space, and have no corner of a room to convert into an art space, then maybe your dining room table could be made into a dual-purpose dining/art table. Just protect the table with newsprint, cardboard or butcher paper when it's in art mode and use a shelf and/or a nearby drawer to store brushes, pencils, paints and art papers. A really nice thing about keeping art supplies visible and handy like this is that they will perpetually remind you of the possibility of spontaneously beginning—and continuing—creative projects of all kinds.

Thank you for picking up a copy of D30. If you made it through most or all of this book's activities, congratulations! I hope you found each of the projects enjoyable and insight-producing. Now that you're finished with the book, consider keeping it in a place where it will readily provide you with ideas for future projects—both personal and professional.

Jim Krause

More Great Titles from Jim Krause and HOW Books

The Logo Brainstorm Book
This helpful book offers multiple approaches for your logo project in an array of styles and themes. Whether you're dealing with monograms, symbols, or a typographic logo, you'll find a wide array of inspiring ideas that you can use as a springboard to finding the right design solution.

The Designer's Ultimate Index
All in one handy carrying case, you'll find three bestselling books from designer, photographer and illustrator Jim Krause. They contain all the inspiration you'll need to come up with brilliant new design solutions. Whether it's working through typography, laying out your page or picking the perfect color, this series covers the bases. It's an amazing tool that can be used on a daily basis in any creative line of work.

Find these books and many others at MyDesignShop.com or your local bookstore.